THE MENDACITY OF HOPE

THE MENDACITY OF HOPE

Barack Obama and the Betrayal of American Liberalism

ROGER D. HODGE

An Imprint of HarperCollins*Publishers*
www.harpercollins.com

HarperCollins books may be purchased for educational, business, or sales promotional use. For information, please write: Special Markets Department, HarperCollins Publishers, 10 East 53rd Street, New York, NY 10022.

FIRST EDITION

Designed by William Ruoto

Library of Congress Cataloging-in-Publication Data

Hodge, Roger D.
   The mendacity of hope: Barack Obama and the betrayal of American liberalism / Roger D. Hodge.
      p. cm.
   Includes bibliographical references.
   ISBN 978-0-06-201126-8
   1. Liberalism—United States.   2. Obama, Barack.
3. United States—Politics and government—2009–
I. Title.
   JC574.2.U6H63 2010
   973.932092—dc22   2010024938

10 11 12 13 14 ID/RRD 10 9 8 7 6 5 4 3 2 1

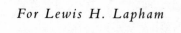

For Lewis H. Lapham

As it is the business of the contemplative statesman to trace the history of parties in a free country, so it is the duty of the citizen at all times to understand the actual state of them.

—JAMES MADISON, "A Candid State of Parties"

Pause, reader, and awfully recollect, that the government is in the hands of speculators.

—JOHN TAYLOR OF CAROLINE, *An Inquiry*

The picture of the prettiest girl that ever lived will in the long run prove powerless to maintain the sales of a bad cigarette. There is no equally effective safeguard in the case of political decisions.

—JOSEPH SCHUMPETER, *Capitalism, Socialism, and Democracy*

CONTENTS

Contents

THE MENDACITY OF HOPE

CHAPTER ONE

THE IDEA OF INFLUENCE

Barack Obama came to us with such great promise. He pledged to end the war in Iraq, end torture, close Guantánamo, restore the Constitution, heal our wounds, wash our feet. None of these things has come to pass. As president, with few exceptions, Obama has merely changed the wallpaper and rearranged the furniture in the White House: his financial policies are in essence those set in motion by George W. Bush, and when it comes to the eternal "global war on terror" he has stealthily embraced the unconstitutional war powers claimed by his predecessor or left the door open for their quiet adoption at some later date. The early executive orders that temporarily warmed the hearts of civil liberties lawyers everywhere were soon eclipsed by slippery and insidious policies that by virtue of superficial changes in tone and presentation have largely avoided damaging publicity.

Obama's director of the Central Intelligence Agency declared that the kidnapping and rendition of foreigners will continue, and the Department of Justice persists in using the Bush administration's expansive doctrine of state secrets against those wrongfully detained and tortured by our security forces and allies. Obama has adopted military commissions, once considered an unpardonable offense against our best traditions, to prosecute terrorism cases in which legitimate convictions cannot be obtained; when even such mock trials provide too much justice, he will make do with indefinite detention. If, by some slim chance, a defendant were to be found not guilty, we have been assured that the president's "post-acquittal" detention powers would then come into play. The principle of habeas corpus, sacred to candidate Obama as "the essence of who we are," no longer seems so essential to a president who maintains secret prisons hidden from due process, judicial and congressional oversight, and the Red Cross. Waterboarding has been banned, but other forms of torture, such as sleep deprivation, prolonged isolation, and force-feeding, continue—as do the practices, which once seemed so terribly important to opponents of the Bush regime, of presidential signing statements and warrantless surveillance.

The rule of law has not been restored; it has been perverted. What had been outlawed but committed, the law now simply permits. Obama's lawyers, benefiting from Bush-era litigation and recent craven legislation, can claim conformity with law, but the disgraceful policies continue largely unchanged. Better, more sophisticated legal arguments obtain for acts that should give any decent human being nightmares. Our torturers and war criminals and illegal spies and usurpers remain at liberty, unpunished. The wars of choice continue and threaten to spread, while some 100,000 soldiers and at least that many private contractors attempt, as Obama so delicately put it, "to finish the job" in Afghanistan's graveyard of empires and our flying robots bomb villagers in the mountains of Waziristan. This, we are told, is progress.

Admirers of the president embrace actions they once denounced as criminal, or rationalize and evade such issues, or attempt to explain away what cannot be excused. That Obama is in most respects better than George W. Bush, John McCain, Sarah Palin, or Joseph Stalin is beyond dispute and completely beside the point. Obama is judged not as a man but as a fable, a tale of moral uplift that redeems the sins of America's shameful past. Even as many supporters begin to show their inevitable displeasure with his policies or his job performance and his poll numbers decline, to his liberal supporters the character and motivations of the president remain above question. *He is a good man. I trust him to do the right thing.*

It is no surprise that innocent children, naive European prize committees, and professional Democratic partisans continue to revere the former heroic candidate, despite everything he has done and left undone. Nor is it surprising that the Republican Party and the broken remnants of the old white supremacy coalition hate and fear the man and will oppose him without quarter (excepting, of course, his war and torture policies, which flatter their nationalist impulses).

Puzzling, however, is the fact that the president, who until recently was an obscure striver in Chicago's Democratic machine, continues to inspire perfervid devotion among many intellectual liberals who know their history. Even they say: Be patient. Give him time. It's hard to change the government. Or, more cynically: He's the best we can do. Thus, his most knowledgeable admirers assume the burden of Obama's sins, bite their tongues, and indulge the temptation to frame his shortcomings as America's own. Obama is not to blame; we are to blame. Obama has not failed us; America has failed him.

If there is a sense in which we the people have failed, it is not that we have neglected to live up to Obama's ideals, his great and historic hopes to bring change to Washington. If we have failed, it is because we have abdicated our sovereign duties in the naive hope that a redeemer would come to deliver us from politics and thus from history.

Americans dislike politics; we take every opportunity to denounce politicians and government bureaucrats even as we pay elaborate homage to the transcendent virtue of the American system of government. One reason for this political schizophrenia is no doubt the substantial gap between the mundane realities of our hopelessly corrupt political system and our ideological image of it. Every political regime, no matter how debased, has its sacred narratives, its myths, dogmas, and tales of glory that are designed to reproduce loyal subjects. America's mythological narrative concerns *democracy*, and that narrative is as distant from reality as it is from James Madison's vision of the republic he helped to establish. Our scriptures are the Declaration of Independence, the Constitution, and a loose canon of essays and letters by the founding fathers, our national saints, who are treated by the faithful as if they acted and spoke with one mind. As with the Bible and the New Testament, of course, most Americans revere our sacred texts without bothering to study them or to achieve basic competence in their interpretation.

According to the conventional theory that appears in our civics textbooks, modern democracy is a political system under which the people decide how they wish to be governed by electing representatives who carry out their will. The ultimate source of authority in the democratic system is thus the sovereign voter, whose solemn and heroic responsibility we celebrate at every national, state, and local election. The basic premise of the conventional view is that the people rule, and so we are told ad nauseam from the time we enter kindergarten—and that, we tell one another at every opportunity, is what makes America the greatest nation in the history of the world.

In our democratic system, the most wonderful system that ever was (the light of nations, the shining city on the hill), the people deliberate over policies and weigh alternatives and come to rational decisions about the public good. In this way we produce what philosophers call the general will, which we communicate (as if by magic or at least by poll) to our elected representatives, who are obliged to carry it out. Even in the face of daily proof that this state of affairs does not exist, the idea that *the people* somehow rule persists as the first article of our civic creed. All who participate in American politics must publicly confess their democratic faith, no matter what their partisan orientation.

All creeds have their rituals, and central to ours is the national election. Oddly enough, a vital component of the electoral liturgy is the traditional observation that our democracy is broken. Viewed from within the mythological narrative, it is. But if we step outside the sacramental theater things begin to take on a different color, and it becomes difficult to argue that the system isn't working. The question is: *for whose benefit* is the system working? Toward the end of answering that ancient and venerable question it might be useful to have before us a more realistic model of our political decision making, a model of what *exists* as opposed to what we *believe*. Perhaps some detachment from sentimental pieties about popular sovereignty might eventually lead to more effective political action on the part of citizens. It might also be of some assistance in understanding the relentlessly pragmatic policies of Barack Obama.

IN KEEPING WITH THE PERVASIVE commercialism that characterizes our society, it is no accident that an economic model of democracy has taken hold. One such account of modern democractic politics was put forth in the 1940s by the economist Joseph Schumpeter, who argued that democracy is best understood as a method of political decision by which individuals acquire the power to rule through a competitive struggle for the people's vote. Far from being a system in which the people rule, Schumpeter maintained, our democracy is best characterized as "the rule of the politician"; the role of the people is simply to accept the leadership of the most successful politicians. Political parties and the coalitions of pressure groups they comprise engage in a constant struggle for power that at certain intervals becomes institutionalized and legitimated by the people's vote. Actually existing democracy, whether we like it or not, has little in common with the ideal of Englightenment philosophers or the ancient variety practiced by Athenian slaveholders. It is no coincidence that democracy as we know it began to arise at the moment when the bourgeoisie was freeing itself from feudal lords and giving birth to capitalism. Businesses seek profits by producing goods and attracting customers; democratic politicians seek power by manufacturing policies and legislation, which in turn attract votes.

This model conforms rather well with the American system that has developed since the Civil War; but as the political scientist Thomas Ferguson has argued for decades, it elides one crucial element, the profound intimacy of business and government. Businesses, especially large corporations, have long recognized that politics is an extraordinarily lucrative market and that political investment (in the form of lobbying, campaign contributions, and other forms of bribery, both legal and illegal) often yields returns that are unmatched elsewhere in our economy. The most advanced businesses thus seek profits by investing in politicians, who manufacture policies to order in return for contributions, which are then used to shape public opinion and attract votes. The relationship

is one of reciprocal predation: politicians and political investors feed off each other as they pursue their different, but not
incompatible, ends. Sometimes, as in the case of billionaire
politicians such as Ross Perot and Michael Bloomberg, lines
become so blurred that it is hard to tell where investment
ends and politics begins. Of course, politicians also continue
to craft policies designed to attract votes, but pleasing the
electorate has increasingly been subordinated to what Walter
Lippmann long ago called the manufacture of consent, and
old-fashioned vote-buying programs are modest in comparison with those designed by and for powerful corporate lob-
bies. Generally speaking, in the marketing of both political
and consumer goods, human emotion is the primary matériel,
as advertising and propaganda play on the public's desires and
fears, exploiting its insecurities and vanities. Both corporations and politicians seek monopolies within their respective
markets, and the consumer-citizen occupies a decidedly re-
ceptive position. The controlling factor, in politics as in business, is often the investor or bloc of investors that supplies the
capital which makes everything possible. Politics, we might
say, is the continuation of business by other means.

Consequently, the most important field of battle in
American democracy is pecuniary, and the primary constitu-
encies of the parties—their most important markets—are not
so much voters, though of course voters are an essential part
of the power equation, but coalitions of business interests.
The conventional view of the American two-party system as
a contest between a party of business and a party of the people, a view perpetuated daily in the marketing of the parties

themselves as well as in the purportedly independent news media, is worse than false; it actively conceals the true nature of the system.

Also conventional in political commentary is the interminable parsing of the ineffabilities of presidential charisma. Franklin Roosevelt is a classic case, as is Barack Obama. The latter's victory over John McCain was attributed to his innate brilliance, his ability to play a long game, also frequently described as a supernatural affinity for eleven-dimensional chess. A somewhat more likely, if insufficiently mystical, explanation was the fact that the economic crisis provided a September surprise that no incumbent party would have been able to survive; historically, a recessionary economy at election time usually signals a partisan turnover. Even without the crisis, of course, there is the matter of Obama's overwhelming fund-raising advantage.

Our leading pundits, however, prefer to portray such victories in terms of character and leadership. These atmospheric intangibles are no doubt important; an appealing candidate is certainly a necessity, especially in our media-polluted era, but the absolute condition not only of success but of simple participation in the political game is a motivated set of investors who are willing to finance the high costs that our system imposes on political participation—costs that for most individual citizens are insurmountable. In the American system the two major parties are best distinguished by their differing coalitions of business interests, though there is often considerable common ground in the vital center, that large set of policies about which the parties and their investors have no significant points of disagreement and over which they engage, at most, in symbolic and empty competition. Over time, these interests tend to shift and evolve, and new alignments and party systems come into being and pass away.

The New Deal system, which prevailed from the mid-1930s until it began to collapse in the 1970s, provides a good illustration. In American legend, the New Deal was imposed at a time when the two-party system divided decisively along class lines, with the Democrats assuming their old banner as the party of the common man and the Republicans mounting a rearguard action as the party of business. Yet it can be argued that the Democratic coalition forged by Franklin Roosevelt was in the most important sense not one of voters, who might well have voted for a compelling chimpanzee rather than Lord Hoover, but of investors. In this view, the core of Roosevelt's investment bloc was composed of capital-intensive, internationally oriented firms; investment banks, including Lehman Brothers and Goldman Sachs, lined up behind the New Deal in opposition to the House of Morgan. Soon after the election, these firms together with non-Morgan commercial banks, such as Chase National, moved to neutralize Morgan's dominance of American finance by securing the Glass–Steagall Act 1933, which divorced investment from commercial banking. Eventually, a grand coalition emerged comprising the investment bankers and other internationalist and capital-intensive firms such as Standard Oil, General Electric, IBM, Zenith, Sears Roebuck, Pan Am, and United Fruit. The legislation that resulted was a powerful brew of labor protection, free trade, and social welfare.

The Republican coalition—protectionist and labor-intensive industries such as textiles, the Morgan interests, and the chemical industry—was outmaneuvered and outmatched. Roosevelt's backers received excellent returns on their investments, and the popularity of the New Deal legislation, which though far from perfect was extremely popular with voters and political investors alike, resulted in forty years of Democratic dominance.

Barack Obama, as the leader of a national party, also stands at the head of a loose coalition of investors, whose interests he naturally tends to serve. This is not a matter of conjecture or speculation; it is one of the most objective of all political metrics: campaign finance and other mediums of political patronage are by their very nature quantifiable. Nor, I hasten to point out, is the idea that politics reflects fundamental economic interests a particularly leftist point of view. The perspective, as the historian Charles Beard pointed out many years ago, is Madisonian: "The most common and durable source of factions," Madison wrote in *The Federalist* No. 10, "has been the various and unequal distribution of property. Those who hold and those who are without property have ever formed distinct interests in society. Those who are creditors, and those who are debtors, fall under a like discrimination. A landed interest, a manufacturing interest, a mercantile interest, a moneyed interest, and many lesser interests, grow up of necessity in civilized nations and divide them into different classes, actuated by different sentiments and views. The regulation of these various and interfering interests forms the principal task of modern legislation, and involves the spirit of

THE MENDACITY OF HOPE

party and faction in the necessary and ordinary operations of government."

Interest is one of the guiding political concepts of the lawmakers who drafted our Constitution, and, despite being enshrined as a sort of capitalist fetish by the worshippers of the divine and invisible hand of the all-seeing, all-powerful Market, the concept has lost much of its currency as the decades have passed into centuries and the American people have forgotten the substance of the founders' insights into political behavior. Despite ritual denunciations of special interests, Madison's concept of interest is undervalued and underutilized, and yet it has lost none of its intrinsic value. The liberal republicans who fashioned our system of government—and then immediately set upon one another, with a savagery that far surpasses the anodyne disputations of our cable television spectacles, in a partisan war to define the meaning and course of republican governance—were not sentimental. They were simply determined to take humanity as they found it rather than as they wished it to be.

The overriding concern, not only of the Federalists who supported the adoption of the new constitution but of the anti-Federalists who opposed it, was the preservation of liberty. In the tradition in which they thought and argued, liberty was considered to be created and possible only in a well-regulated republic. In the Atlantic republican tradition that informs our Constitution, the state, through its laws, creates liberty. The question of the good, which necessarily entails interest, was left to politics, and not by accident. In the essays that form our Constitution's most important commentaries, Madison argues that the federal government would necessarily be a site of clashing interests, with powers distributed among its various compartments to ensure that no one interest might achieve preponderance or dominion over the rest—in other words, to ensure that the good of one class might not be imposed on all others. Interests and thus factions and parties, classes and social groups must necessarily come into conflict and make their demands known. Adding to the complexity, of course, was the curiously divided sovereignty that was constructed so that individuals were citizens of both the particular states and the larger national union, both of which derived their legitimacy from and acted directly upon the people. One of Madison's chief concerns was the creation of a republic that would be large enough to contain the inevitable strife and neutralize the ability of any one self-interested faction to subordinate the purposes of the state to its own, which was the very definition of corruption. As every educated member of the revolutionary generation was well aware, all republics through history had eventually fallen into corruption, devolving into one form of despotism or another; Madison was determined to design a new republic that would, by virtue of a sound constitution, persist in civic health beyond the historical norm. He wished, contrary to all known precedent, to make an immortal republic. Unfortunately, he did not succeed.

Despite our high technology and imperial airs, our low fidelity to the insights of that unrivaled generation of American political thinkers—and particularly to the insights of James Madison—has served us poorly. One need not attempt to reconstruct a strict Madisonian system; nor are we compelled by some law of nature to adhere in the twenty-first century to the views of a collection of eighteenth-century politicians, no matter how brilliant. The proof-texting of simpleminded Founding Father idolaters is no less objectionable than the literalism of ahistorical Christians who believe that Jesus of Nazareth actually raised Lazarus from the dead, walked on water, and rose up on the third day, because the Bible tells me so. True religion no more requires silly magical thinking than republican politics entails worship of the founders. If I attend to the writings of James Madison in particular, it is because he is the chief architect and theorist of our Constitution; the point is to grasp the principles that were meant to animate our political system at its founding, and to see how thoroughly they have been perverted. It may even be that some of them are still useful.

The mundane corruption of our capitalist democracy (a term that nicely, if accidentally, captures the obscene intimacy of big corporations and big government) is not inevitable, and it certainly in no way corresponds to the vision of republican government set forth in our founding documents. Yet despite the stupefying quantities of cash that pollute our politics, we persist in pretending that the money doesn't really matter, that the *less than 1 percent of Americans* who contribute at least $200 to politicians, and especially those who organize and channel those contributions to parties and candidates, do not receive direct returns on their investments. For far too long the American people have been cajoled into believing and acting as if the great mass of the citizenry were an indivisible whole, with one overarching national interest that just happened to correspond with the most profitable environment for the nation's largest and most powerful businesses. The interests of the superrich are not identical with those of the middle classes, and vigorous assertion of the latter's interests, even if they impinge upon those of the former, is very far from being some kind of Marxist class warfare. Such assertion is a legitimate application of republican principles.

Madison could not have foreseen the radical transformations that have overtaken our society in the last 220 years, but in his debates and political battles with Alexander Hamilton, both in the Constitutional Convention and in the years during which the first party system took shape, he could see the outlines of the corruption that has swamped the Constitution. In 1792, Madison published an anonymous essay in the pages of the *National Gazette* newspaper warning of the coming danger. In good republican fashion, he sketched a three-part classification of states, according to what he called the "predominant spirit and principles" of government. What is the animating power that gives life and motion to a regime's activities? The first is a type of government that operates by means of a "permanent military force, which at once maintains the government, and is maintained by it; which is at once the cause of burdens on the people, and of submission in the people to their burdens." Such governments, alas, were the most common and familiar, those "under which human nature has groaned through every age," and that still oppressed most people in most countries—even in Europe, which considered itself the pattern and pride of human civilization. The third, which he recommends and approves, is "a government deriving its energy from the will of the society, and operating by the reason of its measures, on the understanding and interest of the society." Such is the republican form of government, animated by the public interest, the regime "for which philosophy has been searching, and humanity been fighting, from the most remote ages." Madison congratulates his fellow citizens for the glory of having founded such a state.

Yet his well-wishing had come with an edge; his readers knew that the noble regime was in danger, because Madison had just told them so, since before concluding his essay with the exhortation that "her happiness be perpetuated by a system of administration corresponding with the purity of the theory," Madison had devoted by far the longest portion of his typology—and the delivery of this ominous definition was the clear motive for the essay—to a second form of government, that "operating by corrupt influence; substituting the motive of private interest in place of public duty; converting its pecuniary dispensations into bounties to favorites, or bribes to opponents; accommodating its measures to the avidity of a part of the nation instead of the benefit of the whole; in a word, enlisting an army of interested partisans, whose tongues, whose pens, whose intrigues, and whose active combinations, by supplying the terror of the sword, may support a real domination of the few, under an apparent liberty of the many."

Madison's tone is stern and comminatory, and no reader at the time could fail to detect the object of his attack or his clear effort to associate the Hamiltonian program with the corrupt financial machine of English ministerial governance, the pernicious engines of national debt, executive patronage, and standing armies, which to Americans schooled in the rhetoric of English opposition polemics were the unmistakable characteristics of civic corruption and tyranny. This was the rhetoric of the American Revolution, which had been triumphantly completed just a few short years previously with the adoption of Madison's Constitution, and it was now being applied implicitly to the administration of its great war hero, George Washington. "Such a government, wherever to be found, is an impostor," Madison continues. "It is happy for the new world that it is not on the west side of the Atlantic. It will be both happy and honorable for the United States, if they never descend to mimic the costly pageantry of this form, nor betray themselves into the venal spirit of its administration."

Few Americans today—whether they profess loyalty to one of our dominant parties or like many Americans simply pull the lever for what appears to be the lesser evil—should be able to read Madison's definition of government by corrupt influence without experiencing a shudder of recognition. No candid citizen can reasonably maintain that we now live under "a government deriving its energy from the will of the society," or that it operates in our broadest public interest.

Today, after the crash of a speculative bubble of unprecedented proportions, 12 percent of American mortgage holders are delinquent or in foreclosure, real unemployment is at levels unseen since the Great Depression, members of Congress complain of threats from health-care extremists, and state governors are being menaced by right-wing militias. Politicians mutter about nullification and secession and claim to see a tyrant in the White House, while alarmed Democrats detect white robes hidden beneath the colonial costumes of Tea Party demonstrators. Fiscal conservatives look aghast at the rising budget deficit and fear the inevitable coming of hyperinflation, and the good liberals who populate the Democratic base gnash their teeth in despair as the reformist hero they thought they had elected in 2008, amid promises of fundamental change and national renewal, stands revealed after more than a year in office as a common politician with feet of clay. Obama's most extremist enemies see him as an agent of the devil come to steal our liberties, a counterfeit American who was born in some foreign land, a socialist, a communist, an Arab. Obama's supporters strive to keep the faith, but their smiles have begun to harden and grow brittle. Perhaps they cannot bear to let go of the intoxicating and exhilarating illusion that a great man had arrived to set the world aright. The president's most devoted followers tell us that he is just one man, that it's hard to change the government, that he is doing the best he can. Give him time, they say; what do you expect him to accomplish so soon? They point to his achievements: the new health-care law, an arms-control treaty with Russia, the stimulus package, and the rescue of the banks. Some believed that Barack Obama had come to restore the Constitution, to return our nation to the righteous path. A new, glorious era in American politics was at hand. If only that were true. We all can taste the bitterness now.

By the end of Obama's first year in office, after a decisive election victory, with not only a majority in both houses of

Congress but a supermajority of sixty votes in the Senate, the Democrats in their search for the elusive will-o'-the-wisp of bipartisan consensus had squandered both the goodwill of the general public and the political momentum behind their signature initiatives. The stimulus package, too small to begin with and watered down with unstimulating tax cuts and payoffs to political contributors, failed to offer enough relief. Although Main Street continued to bleed jobs, Wall Street had largely returned to profitability, and that was enough for the White House. The Democrats' absurdly misconceived and porcine health bill came very near to perishing after a year's difficult gestation; what passed into law was in some ways the worst of all possible outcomes, a monopolist's dream, a pseudo reform of mind-bending complexity. Stripped of almost all redeeming qualities, without even a token public plan to offer hope of deliverance from the insurance trusts, the Patient Protection and Affordable Care Act could well deliver Congress into the shaky hands of the Republican Party.

Climate legislation was going nowhere; even the administration's preferred approach to carbon emissions, an elaborate and ineffective financial confection formerly known as cap and trade, seemed destined to languish in congressional limbo. Most dramatically, the Deepwater Horizon catastrophe in the Gulf of Mexico demonstrated Obama's unwillingness to disturb even the most demonstrably corrupt "public-private partnerships" between government and big business. "It turns out, by the way, that oil rigs today generally don't cause spills," Obama blithely assured the public shortly after he announced his cynical expansion of oil exploration in American waters. "They are technologically very advanced." Eighteen days later, the BP well, which the Obama administration had carelessly approved, exploded. After the full magnitude of the spill became undeniable, Obama remained unwilling to move beyond his increasingly hollow rhetoric to make the case for a substantive transformation of our energy policies.

Meanwhile, our enthusiastic new commander in chief has doubled down in Afghanistan, despite the fact that underwear attacks can originate from any point on the globe. Obama continues to throw American lives and dollars at an unwinnable war, in a strategic backwater, with no plausible criteria of what might constitute victory in that imperial boondoggle. All pretenses that the famous surge accomplished anything of lasting significance in Iraq, or that the Karzai regime is a credible partner in defeating the Taliban, have vanished like smoke after a Predator strike.

A proper understanding of our predicament can follow only from the realization that Obama, on his own terms, has not failed—his change-hope vision was always a mirage. In fact, Obama is doing what he set out to do. He is busy; he is passing legislation; there are accomplishments to which he can point in the hope of gulling the voters once again, never mind that the laws he has given us represent a betrayal of the best elements of American liberalism, those that are productive of liberty and independence. If we are to move forward politically, we must come to terms with the fact that Obama did not come to save American liberalism; he came to bury it. The professed enemies of liberalism should not rejoice, however; there are worse things in life than a new New Deal. Big government, as the Bush years demonstrated, comes in many guises.

Although in the pages that follow I will make much of the role of money in politics, make no mistake about my point of view: all experience and history testify that statesmen are motivated above all by power and glory. Only the most debased and worthless politician is motivated by a lust for mere wealth; money for the true politician is of interest only insofar as it leads to power—and, besides, as all the world knows, wealth follows power as night follows day. The gross anatomy of Barack Obama's investment coalition is not my ultimate end. Above all I am interested in contributing to the recovery and application of a republican model of political analysis that sees corruption as something far more dangerous and pervasive than mere graft. The stupendous scale of our system of legal bribery, with its unrivaled corporate predation on the body of state, points to a degree of corruption that goes to the roots of our collective and individual political identity. It is not only the government that is corrupt. If one wishes a republic to survive a long time, Machiavelli wrote in his *Discourses on Livy*, it is necessary on occasion to return to first principles.

As our president likes to say, let me be as clear as I can be: an insistence on political economics and the corruption of our politics does not rule out the influence of ideas, ideology, political philosophy, morality, or personal conviction. Certainly ideas play a role in our politics, as do ignorance, stupidity, and malice. *Money, at least in the realm of politics, is nothing but an idea; it is the idea of influence.* I would be the last, moreover, to deny that many well-meaning individuals enter public life out of a sincere desire to do good; unfortunately, most of them end up simply doing well. Despite my sometimes harsh criticisms of the character and actions of Barack Obama, I do not believe that he or any other politician, with the exception of Joe Lieberman, acts out of a conscious desire for the bad. The human capacity for self-deception is infinite.

In what follows I will examine both the rhetoric and the reality of Obama's governing strategies, paying particular attention to his political investors, to the ways and means by which their various and interfering interests have manifested themselves in the ordinary operations of government. The tone, in keeping with the spirit of the great republican pamphleteers, will be anything but deferential; you have embarked on a polemical journey and your guide, on occasion, will be rude. Along the way we will set off on historical and theoretical excursions to examine both the productive insights of our republican forebears and the ways they have been exploited for mercenary purposes. The guiding question throughout will be the ancient one. *Cui bono*? This double dative Latin construction means literally, "To whom for the purpose of a good?" A better translation is: "Who benefits?" Or, even better: "Who profits? Whose interests are being served?" The answer to that question is the answer to another: "Who rules?"

CHAPTER TWO

BARACK OBAMA, INC.

The warning signs that perhaps Barack Obama was not what he claimed to be were there from the beginning, though many thoughtful Americans were blinded by their hopes, carried away by their animus against the hated Bush. When Obama arrived in Washington in 2005, he immediately set about organizing a conventional corporate machine. Even a cursory glance at the profile of Obama's campaign contributors could not fail to worry those who were enchanted by his clean-government rhetoric. His top collective donor, classified by employment affiliation, in the 2003–2004 cycle was the University of Chicago—which is no surprise given his background and connections with that institution. Nor should this shock anyone familiar with the tawdry history of

THE MENDACITY OF HOPE

earmarks and other legislative pork that have flowed to univer-
sities over the years. Obama's second most generous investor
was the law firm Kirkland and Ellis, whose lobbying clients
include the Chicago Board of Trade and the Futures Industry Association, a Chicago-based association representing the
derivatives industry, whose board is populated by executives
at firms such as Goldman Sachs, Citigroup, Morgan Stanley, and JPMorgan Chase. Henry Crown and Company, his
third-ranking donor during that election cycle, is an investment firm that owns stakes in the Chicago Bulls, JPMorgan
Chase, real estate ventures, as well as biotechnology and defense contracting. Fourth was Sidley Austen LLP, a law firm
and lobby shop representing pharmaceutical, biotech, finance,
and real estate firms such as MasterCard, General Electric,
Monsanto, Caterpillar, Bayer AG, and the American Bankers Association. Another important donor was the Exelon
Corporation, a large utility company that owns and operates the largest fleet of nuclear power plants in the country
(and the third-largest such nuclear portfolio in the world). Its
ten power plants and seventeen reactors represent 20 percent
of U.S. nuclear power capacity. From 2004 to 2009, Exelon
spent more than $17 million in lobbying efforts, and several
Exelon executives are among Obama's top fund-raisers. Other
major contributors were the law firm Sonnenschein, Nath,
and Rosenthal; Goldman Sachs; and JPMorgan Chase. Another investor was the law firm Skadden Arps, whose many
lobbying clients include prominent financial firms (Citigroup,
Fidelity), military contractors (Lockheed Martin), insurance
groups, energy companies, and oil companies. Attorneys at
Skadden Arps also raised money for the campaign.

We also know that Obama aligned himself early on with the political economics of Robert Rubin, a former top executive of both Goldman Sachs and Citigroup, whom he first met during his senatorial campaign. This connection was made evident in Obama's hiring of Karen Kornbluh, who worked for Rubin when he was Treasury secretary under President Bill Clinton, as his policy director. Obama also gave the keynote speech at the launching of Rubin's Hamilton Project, a policy group based at the Brookings Institution. The full significance of Obama's embrace of Rubinomics would be clear soon enough.

In a number of key legislative battles, Obama sent unmistakable signals that he was open for business. In 2006, for instance, he voted for enormous loan guarantees for energy companies, guarantees that exposed the government to billions of dollars in losses if those companies were ever to default on their obligations—and that directly benefited Exelon, one of his most significant patrons. Following a controversy in Illinois over undisclosed leaks from nuclear plants, Obama made a great show of criticizing Exelon and introduced legislation mandating stricter disclosure laws. Later, during his presidential campaign, he bragged that the bill had become law; in fact, Obama had watered down his own bill after meeting with Exelon's representatives. Eventually the bill died of neglect. As we have seen during the elaborate shadow play surrounding the financial reform bill, this would not be the last time that Obama engaged in limited tactical assaults on his closest political investors. After Obama ascended to the presidency, Exelon joined the FutureGen project, a titanic clean-coal boondoggle that was hatched in the notorious secret energy-sector meetings presided over by Dick Cheney in the early years of the Bush administration. As part of the American Recovery and Reinvestment Act, otherwise known as Obama's stimulus package, FutureGen received what might be the largest earmark in history, worth $2 billion.

Obama also helped pass the Class Action Fairness Act, which pushed class-action lawsuits out of state courts and into the federal system, where they are less likely to succeed; and he voted to expand NAFTA into Peru. He voted against capping credit-card interest rates at 30 percent, and he opposed the Hardrock Mining and Reclamation Act of 2007, which would have rolled back subsidies for private mines on public lands. Senator Obama, like many midwestern politicians, was also a consistent and forceful advocate of ethanol, the enormously wasteful and inefficient biofuel that enriches members of the powerful Illinois corn lobby, particularly Archer Daniels Midland, the agribusiness giant based in Decatur, Illinois. In 2006, Obama even joined Governor Rod Blagojevich of Illinois in demanding a federal investigation into whether oil companies were illegally discouraging gas stations from offering E-85, a fuel containing 85 percent ethanol.

Nor were all the junior Illinois senator's unsavory votes and positions confined to positions that his corporate backers might find congenial and profitable. Throughout his presidential campaign, Obama trumpeted his opposition to the war in Iraq, particularly the speech he gave in 2002, when he was still a state senator, denouncing the impending invasion. When he arrived in the U.S. Senate, however, he was suddenly much more nuanced. Given multiple opportunities to take a stand, he repeatedly demurred. Unlike some of his less dashing colleagues or Senator William Fulbright during the Vietnam War, Obama made no bold idealistic assaults on the authorization of war funding—nor did he demand the immediate withdrawal of troops. Indeed, the freshman senator, though very busy with a host of small initiatives, did little to attract legislative attention, mostly voting with the large Democratic pack that offered Bush minimal and token opposition as he aggressively pursued his agenda of expanding executive power. In his first months in office, Obama voted to confirm Condoleezza Rice as secretary of state, for Michael Chertoff as the head of homeland security, and for John Negroponte as director of national intelligence—despite Rice's role in the fraudulent campaign to invade Iraq, despite the civil liberties abuses that Chertoff sanctioned after September 11, and despite Negroponte's well-documented association with death-squad activities in Latin America during the Reagan years. Notoriously, Obama supported his aggressively pro-war Senate mentor, Joe Lieberman, in Lieberman's 2006 primary race against Ned Lamont and then refused to campaign for Lamont after Lieberman declined to accept the judgment of Democratic voters. Indeed, Obama's senatorial record, and later presidential positioning, were best summed up in an interview he gave to the *Chicago Tribune* in July 2004: "There's not that much difference between my position and George Bush's position at this stage. The difference, in my mind, is who's in a position to execute."

Obama, at least, unlike his two immediate predecessors, did not have the opportunity to execute mentally retarded murderers to prove his down-home manliness, but he did vote to reauthorize the USA Patriot Act, and in July 2008, in the midst of an embarrassing sequence of reversals and flip-flops, he voted in favor of the Republicans' FISA bill—a bill that he had earlier promised to filibuster—that retroactively blessed the Bush administration's warrantless and manifestly felonious surveillance of the telephone conversations and e-mail traffic of millions of American citizens. The measure also extended legal immunity to phone companies that participated. This vote produced a flurry of hand-wringing from supporters, but the tempest soon passed.

Of course, Obama's vote would not have been decisive in any of these matters—the point is that his behavior was precisely what one would expect from a member of a supine party of pseudo opposition that reveled in giving George W. Bush everything he asked for. Given Obama's obvious presidential ambitions, it was also no doubt important for him to signal his party, and the potential Democratic donors who would be so important in legitimizing his presidential campaign, that he was no firebrand. Again, nothing here is particularly unusual for a member of the Democratic Party; indeed, Barack Obama's senatorial career was undistinguished and conventional. He was considered a Democratic loyalist, a mostly dependable rank-and-file party hack who also happened to be uncommonly eloquent. He was more than willing to engage in the standard horse-trading that goes on in any legislative process and was happy to take positions, such as his stance on ethanol, that were transparent payoffs for major local industries. Yes, he supported a number of modest, anodyne, and

harmless reforms, particularly of campaign finance and lobbying, but nothing so austere that it might seriously impair his
ability to raise cash or keep his backers satisfied. As a legislator
Obama was at best a mediocrity, though in fairness his career
in the Senate had only begun. As a campaigner, however, he
was exceptional, and not only with regard to voters.

BARACK OBAMA, ALL AGREE, WAS an unusual presidential
candidate. Significantly more intellectual than the politicians
we have grown accustomed to in recent years, an eloquent
and attractive man with a lovely family, Obama arrived in
Washington as if by magic. After three terms in the Chicago state senate, with no significant political liabilities despite his years of close association with the Daley political
machine, Obama benefited from remarkably good luck in
his opponents (more than one Democrat felled by scandals in
the primary, the lunatic right-wing berserker Alan Keyes in
the general election) and waltzed into Congress. His famous
speech before the 2004 Democratic national convention had
made him a national figure, and MSNBC's Chris Matthews
immediately predicted that Obama would be America's first
black president. He was an instant political celebrity who
could attract crowds just by walking down the street. Obviously, though, it wasn't just the speech itself, which sounded
his signature themes of consensus, clean government, and
vague hopes for indefinite change; what was perhaps most
telling about Obama's debut performance at the convention

is the degree to which it overshadowed those of John Kerry and John Edwards. Millions of people were forced to confront just how monumentally phony were the politicians who led the Democratic ticket that year. Obama seemed to be saying everything that Americans—or at least the large portion of the country disgusted with what Bush and his minions had wrought in our morally devastated "homeland"—wanted so desperately to hear.

In retrospect, it is obvious that Obama was running for president from the moment he arrived in Washington, especially considering the fact that his best-selling book, *The Audacity of Hope: Thoughts on Reclaiming the American Dream*, which he apparently sold on the day he was elected senator, for almost $2 million, was published in 2006. It is a book written by a man on his way up, a manifesto that makes little sense outside the context of a presidential campaign—and a book-length elaboration of the 2004 convention speech, which had been his national audition before the real powers inside the Democratic Party.

In that first command performance, in subsequent speeches, and in *The Audacity of Hope*, Obama developed a consistent message that he was committed to forging "a different kind of politics," a politics of unity and brotherhood and hope and optimism about the chances of giving every child in the United States a decent shot at a good life, a dignified job with good health care and a reasonable expectation of a secure retirement. He lamented the influence of lobbyists in Washington and their ability not only to pay for access but to cut secret deals and get special treatment and even to write legislation governing their own industries. At a summit on lobbying reform in 2006, he gave a speech decrying the "Washington that's only open to those with the most cash and the right connections." He said that the American people had tired "of a political process where the vote you cast isn't as important as the favors you can do. And they're tired of trusting us with their tax dollars when they see them spent on frivolous pet projects and corporate giveaways." He alluded to the Jack Abramoff scandal and observed that the number of registered lobbyists had doubled since George W. Bush was inaugurated. He noted that lobbyists had spent more than $2.1 billion lobbying Congress in 2004, and he figured that this came to $4.8 million per member of Congress: "$4.8 million per member so that oil companies can still run our energy policy and pharmaceutical companies can still raise our drug prices and special interests can still waste our tax dollars on pet projects." Obama declared that it was time to clean up Washington and return government to the people who don't have an extra couple of million dollars to spend to make sure that Congress looks out for their interests.

Those were mighty fine sentiments. Judging from his speeches and from similar—in fact, almost identical—passages in his book, Obama appeared to understand the dangers of the corruption that was so obviously eating away at our venerable old republican institutions. His rhetoric was so inspiring that sometimes it recalled the language of trust-busting progressives or even the Jacksonians, with their hatred of the Bank of the United States. So it seemed, judging from his speeches—though of course Obama was also quick to point out that "people shouldn't lump together those of us who have to raise funds to run campaigns but do so in a legal and ethical way with those who invite lobbyists in to write bad legislation." Even legal fund-raising had its pitfalls and dangers, Obama would point out in other contexts. He complained about the need to spend four or five hours at a stretch making phone calls to Democratic donors. He seemed genuinely to be in favor of serious campaign-finance reform, and he called the influence of money in politics the "original sin of everyone who's ever run for office." So, yes, judging from his writings, Obama was a man who not only wanted to bring people together but wanted to take money out of the political equation.

Would it be churlish to point out that he didn't really mean it? It may well be that a politician like Obama really believes what he's saying when he mouths platitudes about being a uniter, not a divider; cleaning up Washington; and expelling the special interests and the lobbyists. We'll never know for sure, though a good methodological rule for realist political analysis, by the way, is that one should try as far as possible to bracket discussion of motivations and other intangibles and focus instead on behavior, on what a political actor—whether an individual politician or a great power—actually does. Action, as they say, is the ultimate proof of principle. Of course one can never entirely eliminate speculations about motive, or about whether someone means what he says, but the application of the realist method to domestic politics does tend to minimize airy unfalsifiable assertions about what Obama *meant* to do, or *wants* to do, or *dreams* of doing. If a focus on relatively objective measures such as funding and lobbying thus resembles a mechanical or behaviorist approach to power, then the conventional journalistic focus on White House palace intrigue, the courtly politics of manipulation, access, and advice, is more psychoanalytical. The latter is obviously valuable—especially when the courtiers who act as sources reveal more than they intend—but its usefulness is limited by the plain fact of ax-grinding and the tendency of reporters themselves to be corrupted by the enticements of access and the emoluments of exclusivity. Of course, none of this is meant to suggest that we shouldn't pay attention to what a politician *says* about his intentions; on the contrary, speech is a very important form of political action, and analyzing a politician's words is particularly useful when we can discern a sharp disjunction between his public utterances and his behavior.

And it was clear from the start that Senator Obama's fine-sounding clean-government rhetoric did not entirely comport with his actions on behalf of the corporations and lobbyists who took the trouble to invest in his campaign. This is revealing, because not only did he expend a considerable number of words denouncing the transactional politics at which he was so adept; he also made a point of condemning politicians who speak out of both sides of their mouths. "Most of us are wise to the ways of admen, pollsters, speechwriters, and pundits," he writes in *The Audacity of Hope*. "We know how high-flying words can be deployed in the service of cynical aims, and how the noblest sentiments can be subverted in the name of power, expedience, greed, or intolerance." Indeed we do, for such is the way of the world, but could it be that Obama's high-

flying words had been similarly subverted? How can someone
so candid about the ways that pretty language and soothing words so often conceal mercenary agendas possibly not
mean what he says? He seems so sincere. Obama's enemies are
always defined in broad terms, but he is remarkably consistent
about what those enemies are: narrow interests, ideological
minorities, people who seek to impose their will on honest
folks—he is against all these things, as are all decent Americans. Everyone wishes for the good and hates the bad, just like
Socrates and Jesus. The appeal should be universal.

Obama's campaign message hardly varied from this audacious template. Since we all deplore bad things and esteem
good things, let's all get together and have a great big change.
Let's change our politics and our civic life. We can do it if
we try! He hastens to add, however, that he doesn't know
how to accomplish his goals, nor does he have a "unifying
theory of American government." Instead, he offers general-
izations, vague reflections, modest suggestions, and cautious
assessments. What he wants to do above all is to "ground our
politics in the notion of a common good." Surely we can all
agree that a common good is good.

Throughout his writings, both in his books and in his
speeches, Obama's proposals, suggestions, nostrums, and pan-
aceas are all so painfully balanced and fair, so thoroughly safe
and conventional, that his occasional pretense to radicalism
can only strike the close reader as laughable. Obama tells us
that he is "angry about policies that consistently favor the
wealthy and powerful over average Americans." Since he is a
Democrat, he tells us, he's much more likely to agree with the

New York Times op-ed page than that of the *Wall Street Journal*; he believes in global warming, evolution, free speech, and religious freedom—and naturally he's sensitive to the history of racial discrimination in America. Since he's a reasonable man, furthermore, he recognizes that the Democratic Party is not perfect; as a matter of fact, it can be "smug, detached, and dogmatic at times." Like his friends across the aisle, he stands for free market competition and small businesses; he's suspicious of government bureaucrats and lawyers, and he's certainly not one of those blame-America-first people. He reveres the military, hates our enemies, and endorses the idea that poor, desperate people in the inner city are largely to blame—because of "a breakdown in culture"—for their own miserable circumstances.

In what might be seen as an oblique confession, Obama has acknowledged that he sometimes serves "as a blank screen" on which other people project their own views, preoccupations, hopes, and fears. And, foreseeing the inevitable objection, which Hillary Clinton would in fact register, that he is some kind of airy-fairy idealist who won't be willing to fight for what he believes in or stand up to those nasty Republicans, Obama makes clear that he understands that politics is "a full-contact sport," much like his beloved game of basketball; he adds that "sharp elbows" and "the occasional blind-side hit" are things that he not only doesn't mind but, believe it or not, actually relishes.

Like any politician running against an incumbent party, Obama has to offer some criticisms, but he refuses to buy into the notion that the Bush administration was "an evil cabal" or an illustration of "creeping fascism" and points out that surely we have seen worse times in this country—the Alien and Sedition Acts, Jim Crow, slavery—but at the same time, he has to admit, "our democracy has gone seriously awry." One of the harshest things Obama can say about George W. Bush in his campaign manifesto is that the Republicans "cannot govern." Indeed, Obama goes out of his way to be gracious toward a man who exploited a devastating terrorist attack in an attempt to establish a permanent monopoly on political power for his party, a president who on false pretenses led the United States into an insane, never-ending war, who made torture an explicit and proud policy of the United States, illegally spied on American citizens, and abandoned the writ of habeas corpus, one of the foundational principles of republican liberty. Despite these clear acts of tyranny, Obama doesn't "consider George Bush a bad man."

The big problem with the Republicans, according to Obama, is not so much the substance of their policies but their style. He finds their divisiveness offensive and objectionable. Again and again, Obama declares that Americans are frustrated and tired and unlikely to be involved politically "because they understand that politics today is a business and not a mission, and what passes for debate is little more than spectacle." In order to represent these Americans, who are sick and tired of all the "noise and rage and endless chatter," Obama proposes "a different kind of politics." What kind of politics is that? What kind of politics does not involve noise and rage and endless chatter? A politics based on "a common good"—one based on common hopes, common dreams, a politics where civility reigns. Was there ever a time when such a politics existed anywhere on earth? Like so many nostalgic Americans of a certain age, Obama apparently believes that there once was a golden age of bipartisanship in America, an age when senators of different parties socialized with one another, worked together, and put America first. There was once a time when John Warner and Robert Byrd were unfailingly courteous to each other, when Ted Stevens and Daniel Inouye were true friends. Yes, he admits that this consensus was unique, "forged by the Cold War and the Soviet threat," yet even so this was a time that was "less ideological" than ours.

As always with Obama, he salts his paragraphs with caveats and provisos—this was also the time of McCarthyism, he admits—and drops the names of villains like a trail of bread crumbs to show that he is well aware that what he's saying is more or less false, even as he asserts its truth. So although things weren't really so great back then, though some of those gentle, courteous, friendly senators were capable of filibustering civil rights legislation, and though it was the "economic populism of the New Deal" that helped hold the country together during this period (and the New Deal was nothing if not ideological), the way to get back to those good old days is to dispense with ideology, because everyone knows that ideology is bad, even if Obama never really says what ideology is, or why it's bad.

Thus was Obama's general philosophy of government as we knew it at the outset of his run for the presidency. The big national audition speech had been a triumph; he had made it to the Senate; written the big campaign book; and was setting out on the yellow brick road. Democratic voters clearly loved him. Considering the formidable fund-raising abilities that he was already demonstrating by that point, and the quality of the backers he was attracting, it was clear that he had been accepted by the investor class that dominates the national Democratic Party. The results were impressive: against a token candidate who raised a mere $2.8 million, Obama in his Senate race had raised $14.9 million—in his first attempt at national office, in a relatively short time, with significant contributions from out-of-state donors such as Goldman Sachs, JPMorgan Chase, and George Soros. Indeed, 32 percent of his contributions came from out of state. (By contrast, Senator Dick Durban of Illinois raised about $7.8 million during the 1997–2002 election cycle, with 22 percent coming from out of state. And consider another comparison: Senator John Thune of South Dakota spent just slightly less, $14.6 million, to unseat Majority Leader Tom Daschle in 2004.)

As an army of chroniclers has now endlessly related, in newspaper and magazine articles, blog posts and book-length campaign dissections, candidate Obama possessed a star power and charisma that made him seem inevitable. The media fell in love with this well-spoken, brilliant, and beautiful man—he was the Archangel Obama, a politician with a heart of gold, noble and honest, a family man who had the good sense to defer to his wife at all the right moments, a man so smart and yet strangely so sexy. YouTube videos reveled in the Obama-crush phenomenon, and gushing campaign dispatches, about his euphemistic love for "sweet potato pie," appeared in (of all places) the *New York Review of Books*. Even David Broder, the elderly mascot of Washington punditry, developed something of an Obama crush, describing the candidate's standard stump speech in awestruck terms that have been quoted in more than one campaign wrap-up:

> And then, as the shouting becomes almost too loud to bear, he adds the five words that capsulize his whole message and sends the voters scrambling back into their winter coats and streaming out the door: "Let's go change the world," Obama says. And it sounds as if he means it. In every audience I have seen, there is a jolt of pure electric energy at those closing words. Tears stain some cheeks—and some people look a little thunderstruck.

There is unquestionably something magical about a brilliant politician, a person who can move a crowd with words, inspire a weary and defeated people to hope for a better tomorrow. On the campaign trail Obama displayed a great persuasive gift, which as president he has wielded sparingly, as if he fears he might exhaust it. Oratory was not his only talent, however, for while he was reducing audiences to tearful mobs, he was also raising enormous amounts of money, and contrary to the impression given in many news reports, the money was coming in from large as well as small donors. The announcement that Obama had raised $25,661,047 in the first quarter of 2007 impressed opponents, pundits, and other potential investors. Hillary Clinton, who had been

thought to enjoy a substantial fund-raising advantage, reported $26,041,109 in contributions, but this included money
transferred from her senatorial war chest, so Obama had won
the first quarter. *Obama had raised more money than a Clinton!*
And thus, dramatically, he proved his electoral virility. In
that early filing, moreover, we could see further evidence of
the gap between Obama's rhetoric and his financial reality.
Obama's self-imposed rule that he would not accept fund-
raising help from lobbyists was already foundering, since at
least two of his best fund-raisers were registered lobbyists
until the very moment, more or less, when they began raising money for the campaign. One of them, Alan Solomont,
a Massachusetts nursing-home tycoon and former finance
chairman of the Democratic Party, helped raise $35 million
for John Kerry in 2004; Solomont bundled at least $500,000
in donations for Obama. He is now the United States ambas-
sador to Spain. *¡Olé!*

The money kept rolling in, and before long it was clear
that Obama was outperforming not only Clinton but all the
Republicans, sometimes all of them combined. And he was
attracting large donors who had previously been associated
with the Clintons; the Democratic establishment was moving steadily in his direction. Obama triumphed in the second
quarter as well, raising $32.5 million compared with Clin-
ton's $27 million. Among Republicans during that quarter,
Giuliani led with a mere $17 million. As the long money
primary dragged on, Clinton showed some strength, winning
the next two quarters, yet Obama's momentum was strong,
and the Republicans were looking very bad indeed. McCain

raised a mere $5.4 million in the third quarter and did only slightly better in the fourth, when Ron Paul raised almost as much as Obama. By January 31, 2008, however, Obama surged back into the lead, raising $36 million that month, more than Hillary Clinton, Mitt Romney, and John McCain combined. Clinton never recovered, although there were of course certain formal details that had to be wrapped up over the next several months.

In the official, electoral campaign, Obama once again benefited from his luck in opponents. Hillary Clinton suffered from unhappy associations with the failures and traumas of her husband's presidency—her aborted health-care reform proposal, the Whitewater scandal, the humiliation of the Monica Lewinsky scandal, years of sarcastic commentary about her choice of hairstyles—and the perception of many voters that she was mean, petty, nakedly ambitious, shrill. Clinton's campaign, furthermore, was chaotic and suffered from factionalism and intrigue, not to mention fatal strategic errors, most notably the decision to practically ignore the Iowa caucuses.

Senator John McCain was a more formidable opponent in terms of conventional credentials—a war hero with long service in the Senate, a reputedly unconventional Republican whose name adorned the most significant recent campaign-finance reform law—and in other circumstances he might have prevailed, as his relatively strong polling in the summer of 2008 suggested. Obama spent that summer in a strange fog, apparently unwilling to counter the Republicans' savage attacks. But in the end McCain's campaign was also poorly run and erratic, and his ill-considered and impetuous choice of Sarah Palin as running mate, coupled with the September–October surprise of the financial crisis, made his chances poor at best. His lamentable fund-raising abilities didn't help. Faced with Obama's overwhelming financial superiority, McCain had no choice but to submit to public financing, thus limiting his general-election spending to $84 million, which by the end he failed even to use. Obama, on the other hand, raised more than $150 million in September alone, almost half of what John Kerry raised during his entire 2004 candidacy. During the final weeks of the election, Obama added more than $100 million to the $65 million he had in the bank in mid-October. Although the Republican National Committee outraised and outspent the Democratic party during those last weeks, there was no hope that McCain and Palin could defeat the $750 million man.

OBAMA WAS CONSISTENTLY VAGUE WITH his change-hope message, and on the unavoidable substantive issues he bobbed and weaved, depending on the circumstances (though he did repeatedly and consistently promise that his health-care program would include a public option). Concerned about Jewish perceptions that he was anti-Israel, Obama delivered an obsequious speech at a dinner hosted by the American Israel Public Affairs Committee, declaring that "Jerusalem will remain the capital of Israel, and it must remain undivided." Such language has clear meanings in Middle East politics; Obama had effectively endorsed a hard-line position that would render peacemaking with the Palestinians difficult to say the least; confronted with criticism, the campaign simply backed down and said that Obama didn't mean what he had unmistakably said. Obama also shifted back and forth regarding Iran and the question of what threat its nuclear program does or does not pose to the United States. And as we know, candidate Obama promised to end torture, close Guantánamo, end the war in Iraq, and restore America's moral standing in the world. Many of his fervent supporters chose not to hear him when he promised to send more troops to Afghanistan, perhaps assuming that he was being forced to make a false show of toughness and that he didn't really mean what he was saying. Then there was the embarrassing NAFTA incident, in which Austan D. Goolsbee, the senior economics adviser to the candidate, assured Canadians that Obama's heated anti–free-trade rhetoric during the Ohio primary "should be viewed as more about political positioning than a clear articulation of policy plans." The campaign went into full war mode, denying that any such conversation had ever taken place, but of course it had taken place, and Goolsbee, we now know, had spoken the truth.

There was also the matter of Joe Biden, a plagiarist buffoon who famously said that Obama was "the first mainstream African-American who is articulate and bright and clean and a nice-looking guy." It's hard to imagine a more conventional establishmentarian Democrat than Biden, which accounts for the universal glee among Washington insiders that greeted his selection. Biden's qualifications for the job were obvious:

he was the chairman of the Senate Foreign Relations Committee, he was a Roman Catholic, he had gray hair, and he happened to have been a prominent supporter of the appalling USA Patriot Act, of which he many times claimed to be the author. Obama could scarcely have chosen a running mate more revealing of his own true political personality, the one we are still getting to know, unless he had picked his mentor and good friend Joe Lieberman.

But all this was so "insidery." The general public didn't really remember all that much about Joe Biden, except that their favorite candidate had picked him, and he had such a nice big smile. *And, besides, what do you want, Sarah fucking Palin as your vice president?* Victory, when it came, as it had to, was sweet for so many Americans. They danced in the streets. We're still dealing with the hangover.

Not everyone suffers in the same manner, of course. Some of us lose our jobs, our homes, everything we have. Others, notably the principal employees of several large banks who collectively hold assets worth more than 60 percent of GDP, get outsize bonuses whether or not their companies make money. These are the notorious savvy bankers, including some who had the audacity to snub the president of the United States when he summoned them for a face-to-face meeting. One of them was Lloyd Blankfein, the chairman and CEO of Goldman Sachs, also known as Government Sachs, that famous investment bank—now a bank holding company—about which we hear so much in the news these days. How fascinating the way fortune has smiled on Goldman Sachs over the years—at least until the SEC's civil fraud investigation erased $20 billion from its market valuation. How curious that Goldman also seems to have been intimately involved in the still unfolding Greek crisis. A cursory glance at Obama's contributors, organized helpfully by the Center for Responsive Politics according to the individual investor's employer, confirms that Goldman occupies a place of honor. It is, after the University of California, Obama's leading contributor in the 2008 presidential cycle. That list of contributors shows an overwhelming predominance of financial firms, as well as other elite universities. Herewith are Obama's top twenty investors and their cumulative donations, in descending order of generosity:

University of California	$1,591,395
Goldman Sachs	$994,795
Harvard University	$854,747
Microsoft	$833,617
Google	$803,436
Citigroup	$701,290
JPMorgan Chase	$695,132
Time Warner	$590,084
Sidley Austin LLP	$588,598
Stanford University	$586,557
National Amusements Inc.	$551,683
UBS AG	$543,219
Wilmerhale LLP	$542,618
Skadden, Arps	$530,839
IBM	$528,822
Columbia University	$528,302

Morgan Stanley	$514,881
General Electric	$499,130
U.S. government	$494,820
Latham and Watkins	$493,835

It's a very distinguished group. Some of those firms figure prominently on the list for John McCain as well, but Goldman, Obama's top corporate backer, who took a $994,795 stake in his campaign, invested only $230,095 with the Republican candidate. The disparity is striking, isn't it? Obama received more than four times the amount McCain did, and number twenty on Obama's list (Latham and Watkins, $493,835) gave more to him than McCain's most generous investor, Merrill Lynch ($373,595), gave to the Arizona senator. Obama collected almost $44 million from lawyers and lobbyists; the finance, insurance, and real estate sector (appropriately known as FIRE) invested just under $40 million; and the health sector donated $19.5 million. In all, Obama raised $745 million to John McCain's $368 million—more than twice as much.

Given these figures, it's hard to see why anyone thought that McCain and Palin might actually end up in the White House, and given the industry profile of Obama's contributors—high technology, higher education, and high finance—it is hardly surprising that finance has been the predominant focus of the Obama administration's efforts over the last year and a half. Goldman, in particular, received an extraordinary return on its political investment. In 2008 Goldman invested $4,461,988 in Democratic candidates, about 75 percent of its total $5,941,639 in political donations.

The firm gave $1,866,144 directly to the Democratic Party. It gave $1,136,737 to the Democratic National Committee, to which it was the top donor in 2008. Even if we take a longer view, and include everything Goldman has donated to candidates from both parties since 1990—all legally laundered through its employees and affiliated PACs—the sum comes to just under $32 million. In return, Goldman has received untold billions from the federal government—we may never know how much, though if we look simply at what the firm received through the TARP program it made a return of 111,378 percent. Once Goldman received its bank charter from Timothy Geithner, it was able to borrow at near zero interest rates, an enormous subsidy worth tens of billions of dollars a year. Citigroup, like Goldman, owes its survival, during our recent financial difficulties, to the largesse of our representatives in Washington, who declined for some odd reason to exact any significant behavioral concessions in return for their generosity. Its TARP return on investment was a staggering 401,194 percent. Citigroup has spent slightly less on politics over the years and balanced its investment more judiciously between the parties, sometimes giving more to the Republicans. But in 2008, it clearly saw which horse was likely to come in first, and made a 65 percent bet—$3,078,958 out of $4,879,138—on Democrats. Overall, the top corporate donors in the 2008 election were Goldman Sachs, JPMorgan Chase, Citigroup, and AT&T, all of which except AT&T lean toward the Democrats.

Of course, since he is a Democrat, Obama and his party also benefited from substantial contributions from the nation's labor unions. The International Brotherhood of Electrical Workers gave $3,917,821 to Democrats in 2008, the American Federation of Teachers donated $2,836,161, and the Teamsters threw in $2,526,624. Direct contributions, however, don't even come close to capturing how much unions spend in elections. The Service Employees International Union nearly bankrupted itself in its effort to elect Barack Obama, spending roughly $60 million on political activities. It's remarkable to see how little the unions have received in return; clearly not all investors are created equal. The failed Employee Free Choice Act received only nominal and tepid support from the administration; it took more than a year for Obama to finally use a recess appointment to install Craig Becker, a well-regarded labor attorney, on the National Labor Relations Board. Certainly the new government is significantly more friendly to labor than was the Bush administration, but there is no sign that the president will support any fundamental changes to the larger antiunion legal framework that has contributed to the erosion of the labor movement. Since 1965, private-sector union enrollment has declined from 30 percent to about 7 percent. Indeed, the charter schools that Obama and his secretary of education, Arne Duncan, champion are an important element of the national movement to break the teachers unions. Since there is zero danger that labor will shift its political investment to the opposing party, the Democrats have no incentive to make sure that labor receives a return on its investment. Thus unions believe they have no choice but to keep paying for mere crumbs. In a sense, the bailout of the U.S. auto industry, in which the UAW was forced to permit management to liquidate its contractual obligations in return for stock in dying companies, can be seen as the Democratic Party's final severance payment to the labor movement.

Although I have by no means painted an exhaustive portrait of Obama's investment bloc, the profile—in silhouette as it were—of the Democrats' brainy and innovative techno-financial coalition could hardly be more obvious: they are our very own high fliers, the bastard offspring of Alexander Hamilton and the worst nightmares of the anti-federalists and Jeffersonian republicans made flesh.

No sooner had the Archangel settled down in Washington, D.C., than the inconvenient campaign promises began to be shed like worn-out feathers from his downy wings. Reporters and commentators pointed out that his oft-repeated vows to cut lobbyists out of the policy game might be difficult, though experts immediately noted that Obama's new rules contained so many gaps and loopholes that they would be easy to circumvent; John Podesta, who headed the transition team, had worked as a lobbyist, though not in the previous year, and he had lobbied on military spending and energy issues, including biofuels, one of Obama's pet subjects. David Axelrod, Obama's close adviser and chief campaign strategist, was a partner in a public relations firm that represented companies such as AT&T, Household Financial (a subprime lender), and Exelon, one of Obama's big home-state investors. The transition team also included lesser figures with ties to the communications industry, high technology companies, Native American tribes, investment firms, various and sundry lobbyists, utilities, aerospace firms, oil companies, and military contractors. Also, notably, the transition team included John O. Brennan, who was the CEO of a military contracting company and the former chief of staff to the CIA director George Tenet. Even though Brennan was tainted by his association with Bush's torture program, Obama had apparently planned to appoint him as his CIA director. A minor uproar eventually forced him to choose Leon Panetta, Bill Clinton's former chief of staff.

But it was Obama's immediate choice of Rahm Emanuel as chief of staff, practically his first decision as president-elect, that set the tone for all subsequent disappointments and put his most liberal backers on notice that the change-hope agenda was itself undergoing a radical metamorphosis. After that, the decision to put Hillary Clinton in charge of the State Department was hardly a surprise, despite the long nasty primary. Most of the objections to Emanuel took his famously profane and aggressive behavior as their theme, as pundits scratched their chins and wondered how it was that a man promising to change the tone in Washington could choose such a thug to run his administration. Few bothered to point out that toughness was the least of the objections to Emanuel, who, in addition to being President Clinton's point man on NAFTA, has been a leader of the Democratic Leadership Council, the faction of pro-business Democrats that has largely succeeded in shedding what little had remained of the party's old New Deal agenda. Emanuel got his start as a political operative and fund-raiser for Mayor Richard M. Daley of Chicago, who later helped place his protégé in Congress by mobilizing city workers to campaign on Emanuel's behalf. During the 1992 campaign, Emanuel raised money for Bill Clinton while working as a consultant for Goldman Sachs and Richard Daley (auditors later discovered a number of improper entries in the campaign's books) and then raised $25 million for the inauguration. After returning to Chicago in the middle of the Lewinsky scandal, Emanuel took a job as an investment banker with Bruce Wasserstein, of Wasserstein Perella, a major Clinton contributor, and within three years earned $18 million, much of that in deals involving Democratic donors and defense contractors. When he ran for Congress in 2002, Emanuel raised more money from Wall Street than any other congressman—even more than Senator Chris Dodd, who between 1989 and 2009 raised $15,060,922 from the FIRE sector, more than anyone else except John Kerry, Charles Schumer, and John McCain.

Vice President Joe Biden, for his part, named as his chief of staff a former lobbyist whose clients had included Fannie Mae, Time Warner, and US Airways, as well as ImClone (a pharmaceutical company with a somewhat tarnished reputation). It was the nomination of Tom Daschle as secretary of health and human services, however, that created a scandal. To devoted Washington courtiers, Daschle was a perfect pick, a former Senate majority leader who had all the right connections on the Hill, a man who could get things done. For those who cared about honest government, however, Daschle was a perfect petri dish specimen of the cancerous growth of

Washington corruption. Obama considered him a close personal friend. The trouble followed Daschle's filing of disclosure statements revealing what he had been up to in the years since he was defeated in the South Dakota Senate race by John Thune, despite having spent more than $21 million in what was the most expensive congressional race of 2004. Over the previous two years, Daschle had earned more than $5 million, of which $220,000 came from speaking fees paid by the health-care industry; he received $250,000 in director's fees from BP. He was also a board member of the Mayo Clinic and two biofuel concerns, and a paid adviser of Alston and Bird, a lobbying firm that represents many health industry firms, including pharmaceutical companies. His wife, Linda Hall Daschle, a prominent military and aerospace lobbyist, was formerly a high-ranking official at the Federal Aviation Administration, and her clients have included American Airlines, Boeing, General Electric, Lockheed Martin, and Norfolk Southern. It was impossible to imagine a more typical example than Daschle of the revolving door between government and industry, which Obama had, as a candidate, denounced as the "political process where the vote you cast isn't as important as the favors you can do." What killed the nomination, however, was not Daschle's industry ties—Obama stood stubbornly and firmly behind his friend—but the fact that he was the third administration nominee who had turned out to be a tax cheat (one of the others, notably, being Tim Geithner, secretary of the Treasury). Daschle's omission was no mere accounting error, a failure to carry a sum to the next column on some indecipherable federal tax form. No, it turned out that Daschle owed $140,000 in back taxes for the use of a private chauffer that had been provided by a company called InterMedia, the owner of *Soul Train*, which also paid him millions in fees for unspecified "services." The *Washington Post* attempted to find out precisely what Daschle could possibly have done for so much money but learned only that the former senator did "a lot of helpful work."

Tax evasion was certainly the least of Daschle's sins, but that happened to be a traditionally sanctioned disqualification for presidential appointees, even if it had nothing to do with a failure to pay taxes on illegal household labor. What was more disturbing, given the financial crisis that had helped get Obama elected, the most serious such crisis since the Great Depression, was Obama's choice of economic advisers. Optimists had hoped against hope that just maybe Obama would appoint Paul Volcker as secretary of the Treasury, and the true starry-eyed idealists thought that maybe an economist like the Nobel laureate Joseph Stiglitz would be brought in as an adviser. Such wishes were in vain. Obama's fateful decision to appoint Clinton's former Treasury secretary, Robert Rubin's protégé Lawrence Summers, to head his National Economic Council, and Timothy Geithner to be secretary of the Treasury—the president of the New York Federal Reserve Bank, who had worked for both Summers and Rubin (not to mention Henry Kissinger), and who was the prime architect of Bush's bank bailout—demonstrated that yet another president had fallen under the spell of Rubinomics.

CHAPTER THREE

A PARABLE OF PEACHES

Close readers of *The Audacity of Hope* were not surprised. The ambitious senator had dropped Rubin's name in his campaign manifesto during a discussion of his thoughts about the challenges facing the American economy. The passage is classic Obama, and reveals a great deal about his transcendental mojo, but before we can appreciate its full significance, we need to place the passage in its full context. The chapter, entitled "Opportunity," is still the most complete statement of Obama's economic philosophy, such as it is.

An elegant framing device opens the discussion. Obama—having learned to his sorrow that senators are obliged to "fly a lot," and having been informed by his staff that senators are permitted to take advantage of a friendly service offered by affluent well-wishers (who tend to avoid the inconvenience and hassle of commercial airline terminals, the endlessly theatrical and largely ineffective security measures, and the distinct possibility of sitting next to somebody with personal hygiene issues)—decides "to give private jets a try." The opportunities to which the chapter title refers were not simply those provided to a young senator, the perks and privileges of wealth and power, but the opportunities (or lack thereof) of gainful employment being offered to the average Joe who populates those areas of the country that private jets tend to bypass. Shortly after an exciting visit to the headquarters of Google, where he benefited from the insights of Larry and Sergey, "two of the richest people on earth," Obama got into a car and drove down to Galesburg, Illinois, as it happens the same working-class town on the border of Iowa that he had mentioned in his world-famous 2004 convention speech, where a Maytag plant was due to be shut down, leaving 1,600 employees out of work, so that operations could be "shifted" to Mexico. The set piece thus introduced hinges on a well-worn trope of modern political rhetoric—a clear opposition between the world's most dynamic company, conjured out of the ether during the dot-com explosion by force of entrepreneurial will, and an old-line rust-belt manufacturing concern shipping jobs overseas with no thought for the devastated communities left behind.

The only question was what moral would be drawn from this parable of senatorial glad-handing. "You'll get little argument these days," Obama writes, "from either the left or the right, with the notion that we're going through a fundamental economic transformation." Ah, yes, it's true: like pilgrims, we are passing through a dark valley, menaced by economic forces that we can only dimly comprehend. What are these forces? "Advances." Advances, he tells us, are causing disruptions, "advances in digital technology, fiber optics, the Internet, satellites, and transportation." These "advances" have "leveled the economic barriers between countries and continents." Notice how impersonal these advances are. Where did they come from? How did they get here? No one knows! And these advances are not alone; they are joined by "pools of capital." Where did the pools come from? Did they cause the advances or did the advances cause the pools? These pools, he said, were scouring the earth, searching for "returns," and not just any returns; these pools demand the best returns. Pools and advances, aided and abetted by "a few keystrokes," searching for the best returns. How dreadful, how sad, that those Maytag workers down in Galesburg were suffering from the effects of those pools and advances. But take comfort, for these pools and advances, aided by keystrokes and a "flatter" world, scouring the planet for returns, are bringing "significant benefits to American consumers." Ah, benefits. Everyone loves benefits. I once had benefits myself, before I was summarily fired without warning one bright January morning. What kind of benefits have the pools and advances brought us?

Peaches. "Peaches in winter." Peaches in winter, Obama tells us, and big-screen televisions.

Yet Obama reminds us that all is not well. In addition to the tasteless winter peaches and those big flat-screen televisions, which are unquestionably cool, the advances and the pools have caused problems. Don't forget those unhappy soon-to-be-downsized workers in Galesburg. They are proof that the advances and pools have "greatly increased economic instability for millions of ordinary Americans." So, on the one hand, we have Larry and Sergey at Google and their friends the knowledge workers, who know how to handle the advances and the pools—in fact, some of their best friends happen to be advances and pools—and, on the other hand, we have millions of ordinary Americans like those workers down in Galesburg, who face a "future of low-wage service work, with few benefits," but lots of winter peaches, "and the risk of financial ruin in the event of an illness, and the inability to save for either retirement or a child's college education."

What is to be done? That, of course, is the question. In what follows, Obama presents a dizzying series of hands— on the one and then the other, repeatedly, like some hyper-discursive blue-skinned Hindu deity—in which he discusses the Bill Clinton wing of the Democratic Party (the wing to which he belongs, but he doesn't really come out and tell us that), which embraces the new economy of advancing pools, even though "a sizable chunk" of the Democratic base resists the agenda. So it's the pools versus the chunk. The pools and their friends the advances point to "high-value, high-wage jobs." Meanwhile, the sizable chunk (yes, she could afford to lose a few pounds) waits an hour for the bus after she clocks out of work at the big Wall-Mart superstore on the edge of town and finally gets home around 10 P.M. to find her son eating Doritos and watching porn videos on the bedroom computer—while her daughter in the living room taps out text messages on her cell phone as she watches *American Idol* on the flat-screen TV. Contemplating this scene, our sizable chunk of a low-wage worker just looks at the bowl of peaches on her kitchen table and wonders if maybe she'd rather have a better job.

Barack Obama did not consider this.

Next come the Republicans, whom he did consider, who believe that tax cuts, deregulation, and the privatization of government functions and services will solve our problems with the pools and the advances by letting them work more fruitfully and productively in the service of the ungrateful sizable chunk and other hapless workers. According to the Republicans, these faceless forces of globalization have been shutting down factories like that one in Galesburg because the government is imposing too many unreasonable costs on the factory owners. If only the owners didn't have to pay so much in taxes, and if the minimum wage weren't so goddamn high, and the regulations weren't so onerous, then maybe we'd still have those Maytag plants in southern Illinois and people would have even more peaches. The problem with the Republicans, however, is that they cut taxes and deregulated industry and privatized everything they could think of, but they forgot to shrink the government—they forgot to stop spending. (Earmarks, Obama points out, were up 64 percent under Bush, though he doesn't add that this extremely profit-able appropriations technique was invented in the 1980s by Democrats—by former aides to George McGovern). And that continued spending has led to a ballooning deficit and widening inequality; and because of the resulting "sea of red ink" it is more difficult for the government to make the investments needed "to address the economic challenges of globalization." O Lord, now we have to worry about the Red Sea, too.

What we require, therefore, is "a new consensus around the appropriate role of government in the marketplace." We need a *new consensus* on taking "the tough steps" that will make America more "competitive." Competition—from the Chinese, the Japanese, the Indians, the Europeans—is what's killing us, even though our GDP, Obama admits, is bigger than various combinations of our competitors' economies. If America were just more competitive, you see, the advances and the pools wouldn't be able to take away our benefits and the red sea would shrink down to a manageable lake or maybe even a pond.

Consensus is where we want to be. How do we get there? First, we have to understand our history—"how our market system has evolved over time"—so Obama gives us a quick rundown of what might be called the long, slow courtship of big government and big business in America, thereby touching on the essential political debate that has raged throughout American history, the primeval dispute between Hamilton and Jefferson over the fundamental character of the republic. As Obama tells it, the central question of that evolution concerns the role of government in the marketplace, and it begins with Hamilton's allegedly firm understanding that "only through the liberation of capital from local landed interests could America tap into its most powerful resource—namely the energy and enterprise of the American people." Lincoln agreed, Obama tells us, and it was his courageous embrace of the Hamiltonian tradition by making the investments in infrastructure (the transcontinental railroad) and know-how (land-grant colleges) that led to "a fully integrated national economy." Obama's story continues with Teddy Roosevelt, who embraced that tradition of active government, particularly in his determination to intervene vigorously in market failures by busting the trusts; and with Woodrow Wilson's establishment of the Federal Reserve and our first consumer protection laws, the economic counterpart of safe sex. The climax of the tale comes with the towering achievements of Franklin D. Roosevelt and the New Deal: the Securities and Exchange Commission, the FDIC, "countercyclical fiscal and monetary policies," Social Security, the National Labor Relations Act. But the story does not end with FDR. Although there were still, as always, two hands to consider (the right, who feared "creeping socialism"; and the left, who thought FDR was just getting started), Obama claims that Lyndon B. Johnson encountered "only modest political resistance" as he had his way with Congress and enacted his Great Society programs. Finally, it was Richard Nixon (a Republican!) who sired the Environmental Protection Agency and the Occupational Safety and Health Administration.

The guiding light throughout Obama's narrative is the "basic insight" of Alexander Hamilton, "that the resources and power of the national government can facilitate, rather than supplant, a vibrant free market." But there was only one problem with what Obama calls, with tangible condescension, "this liberal triumph": "capitalism would not stand still." Once again we come around to those faceless forces, the pools and the advances, the monstrous progeny of that great beast with two backs, the consummated marriage of business and government—but now, before we tire of the joke and the innuendo and the exclamation points, we can call it by its given name: globalization! Productivity growth, Obama tells us, began to lag; OPEC grabbed a bigger portion of the economy's excess profits; and competition—competition!—from Asian manufacturers, with their cheap domestic labor, began to take its toll. Cheap imports flooded in. Jobs started to migrate overseas, like birds. All these bad things just happened, apparently without any direct human intervention, and certainly not because of policy decisions made by human beings of blood and flesh, officers of the national government, whose Hamiltonian role, after all, is to facilitate a vibrant free market.

Consequently, as a result of globalization, the old "stodgy" corporate model no longer worked. "Steady profits" weren't good enough anymore. Shareholders demanded "more value." Corporations found new methods of increasing productivity—automation, layoffs, offshoring—and "those corporations that didn't adapt were vulnerable to corporate raiders and leveraged buyout artists, who would make the changes for them." An inevitable process, the march of angry promiscuously mixed-up metaphors, the oxymoronic forces of globey globalization and tortilla flatness—all bearing down with impersonal and unappealable power on places like Galesburg, Illinois. It was not, contrary to what you might think, the economic equivalent of rape, which according to Texan political lore you might as well lie back and enjoy. Rather, it was a tsunami, an unstoppable, relentless force. It was nobody's fault. One had to adapt as well as possible, hold on for dear life, or perish.

Business, at least, was adapting to the new "environment," which somehow just sprouted up out of ground, but that was not the end of the story. A great hero was coming, and he would answer the call of the people. "As Ronald Reagan's election made clear," Obama writes, "the people wanted the government to change as well." It is surpassingly odd but true: the consummation of Obama's narrative in this handy-dandy history of the "evolution of our market system," in which history he professes to discover the elements of a "new consensus," is the presidency of Ronald Reagan.

Reagan did have some flaws. Obama admits that Reagan exaggerated the size and scope of the welfare state, but "still, the conservative revolution that Reagan helped usher in gained traction because Reagan's *central insight*—that the liberal welfare state had grown complacent and overly bureaucratic, with Democratic policymakers more obsessed with slicing the economic pie than with growing the pie—contained a good deal of truth." Just as the corporations were "adapting" to change, government would adapt, by shedding obligations and downsizing, because, Obama asserts, some things that government has been doing can be better done more cheaply and efficiently and flexibly by private companies. What things? On this subject, for some reason, he does not offer examples. He further admits that taxes weren't really eliminating people's incentive to work hard and earn lots of money—there were plenty of rich people in America prior to Reagan's tax cuts, "but they did distort investment decisions—and did lead to a wasteful industry of setting up tax shelters." Tax shelters! Not tax shelters! Thank God Reagan did away with the need for tax shelters!

If Reagan was the right-wing messiah to Barry Goldwater's John the Baptist, Bill Clinton was Paul of Tarsus. Although we do not possess the authoritative account of Bill Clinton's conversion on the road to Little Rock, it can with great plausibility be dated to 1980, and perhaps it occurred in the vicinity of Center Street, on that awful night when good Bill suffered defeat in the gubernatorial election against a Republican challenger. Two years later, Clinton was back in the governor's saddle, and before long he was working to wriggle the Democratic Party away from its New Deal base and toward a decidedly more business-friendly position: the "third way." Obama tells us that Clinton's promise for more aggressive government intervention in the economy helped him win the 1992 presidential election. Certainly the recession helped the campaign along, as did the candidacy of Ross Perot. Obama praises Clinton for putting a "progressive slant on some of Reagan's goals," by which he presumably means Clinton's wholesale adoption of the Republican economic agenda, from passing the North American Free Trade Agreement to cutting taxes, gutting the welfare system, embracing the rhetoric of small government, and—a dubious achievement—realizing a federal budget surplus for the first time since 1969. Let us recall that Jesus did not build the church; nor, despite certain traditions, did Saint Peter. It was Paul, the former persecutor of Christians, the turncoat, the apostle to the gentiles, who did more than anyone else to carry the Gospel to the wide world. So it was with Bill Clinton, the former liberal, now rechristened a New Democrat, purveyor of the third way, who truly and successfully evangelized Reagan's Good News about the end of big government and welfare as we know it.

THE PROBLEM WAS THAT "CAPITALISM is still not standing still." No, indeed it was not, and as it happens, if we leave the Archangel Obama for the time being, we can point to two epochal acts of government taken under the Apostle Bill, both of which were championed by Barack Obama's current economic wise men, that directly prefigured capitalism's most recent danse macabre. Those changes were the 1999 repeal of the Glass-Steagall Act by the Financial Services Modernization Act (aka the Gramm-Leach-Bliley Act), which was the perfection of a long series of deregulatory measures that had effectively gutted the spirit of the New Deal market safeguards, and the passage of the Commodities Futures Modernization Act of 2000, which helped ensure that capitalism not only kept moving but broke into a gallop, feral and rampant as it had not been since 1928. Although some financial critics downplay the importance of repealing Glass-Steagall, arguing that regulators had long since abandoned the field, Gramm-Leach-Bliley certainly represents an abject surrender to the spirit of market fundamentalism that led to the crash of 2008, and to a $200 million lobbying campaign. Those regulatory decisions were potentially open to challenge, furthermore, so it was important for the banks to receive the blessing of Congress. Too much money was at stake, and in particular the gigantic merger of Citibank and Travelers Insurance had to be blessed. On November 5, 1999, the *New York Times* described the repeal of Glass-Steagall as "the most important banking legislation in 66 years," and quoted Secretary of the Treasury Lawrence Summers (that's right, Obama's friend Larry) as follows: "Today Congress voted to update the rules that have governed financial services since the Great Depression and replace them with a system for the 21st century. This historic legislation will better enable American companies to compete in the new economy." Senator Phil Gramm, one of the primary sponsors of the bill, was triumphant: "The world changes, and we have to change with it," he said. "We have a new century coming, and we have an opportunity to dominate that century the same way we dominated this century. Glass-Steagall, in the midst of the Great Depression, came at a time when the thinking was that the government was the answer. In this era of economic prosperity, we have decided that freedom is the answer."

Senator Chuck Schumer was similarly bullish on the bill. "If we don't pass this bill, we could find London or Frankfurt or years down the road Shanghai becoming the financial capital of the world," he said. "There are many reasons for this bill, but first and foremost is to ensure that U.S. financial firms remain competitive." Likewise Bob Kerrey, the gentle senator from Nebraska: "The concerns that we will have a meltdown like 1929," he said, "are dramatically overblown." A handful of more sober personages, such as Senator Russell D. Feingold and the late Senator Paul Wellstone, were not so chipper: "Scores of banks failed in the Great Depression as a result of unsound banking practices, and their failure only deepened the crisis," Wellstone told the *Times*. "Glass-Steagall was intended to protect our financial system by insulating commercial banking from other forms of risk. It was one of several stabilizers designed to keep a similar tragedy from recurring. Now Congress is about to repeal that economic stabilizer without putting any comparable safeguard in its place."

The repeal of Glass-Steagall came at the end of a decade of financial scandals and crises—among them the Orange County debacle, the Barings collapse, the Mexican peso bailout, the Asian currency crisis, and the collapse of Long-Term Capital Management—an escalating series of financial train wrecks, each more dangerous than the last to the integrity of the world economy, and all in some way based on financial "innovation." Surely, we had seen plenty of evidence that greater "freedom" was not, in fact, the answer for the banks that had brought us such exotic securities as CMOs, PACs, TACs, VADMs, PERCS, ACES, Z bonds, and the unforgettable FELINE PRIDES.

On October 27, 1999, a week after the Clinton administration and Congress agreed on the terms of the bill, but before it was passed, Robert Rubin—who had resigned as secretary of the Treasury that summer to make way for his protégé Lawrence Summers—accepted a job as chairman of the executive committee at Citigroup, whose merger with Travelers was blessed by Gramm-Leach-Bliley. Rubin told a reporter that he had helped negotiate the compromise between the White House and the Republican Congress, and had been instrumental in making sure that the law preserved the Community Reinvestment Act (CRA), which requires banks to make loans in poor, financially underserved areas, and about which we have heard a great deal during the subprime lending crisis. "I care greatly about CRA," Rubin said. "I did have conversations about that." Both Rubin and Sanford Weill, the second member of the new Citigroup triumvirate (the third was John Reed, who didn't last long in that role), emphasized that they had not discussed the possibility of working for Citigroup while Rubin was Treasury secretary: "It would have been inappropriate," Rubin said, "to discuss that while I was in office."

EVEN MORE SERIOUS WAS THE Commodities Futures Modernization Act, which at the last minute was slipped into an omnibus appropriations bill, passed on the last night of the lame-duck congressional session in December 2000, and signed into law by Bill Clinton. This bill, like the repeal of Glass-Steagall, was also the handiwork of Senator Phil Gramm, and we know that it was supported by Robert Rubin and Lawrence Summers. (Rubin, in fact, as Treasury secretary, intervened repeatedly when the Commodity Futures Trading Commission (CFTC) tried to assert its

oversight in the shadowy derivatives market.) It was the culmination of a long push—driven by the bank lobby—for deregulation that began under Obama's great exemplar, Ronald
Reagan. Back in January 1993, another lame duck—Wendy
Gramm, Senator Phil Gramm's wife, who was the head of
the CFTC—had issued a regulatory fiat declaring that most
"over-the-counter" derivatives were exempt from regulation.
There was no sound regulatory reason for this decision, of
course, because derivatives—so called because their value is
derived from some other asset such as a mortgage or an agri-
cultural commodity—are not functionally different in pure
economic terms from other kinds of financial instruments.
The original purpose of such instruments, as bankers often
tell us to justify their existence, is to hedge against risk: for
instance, the risk of a currency fluctuation, against which one
might purchase options to buy or to sell currency at a particular exchange rate at a particular time; or against the default of
mortgages that have been securitized into a bond, for which a
bank might buy a credit default swap. That's the official doctrine, the one put out for public consumption, and according
to the Commodities Exchange Act, traditional derivatives,
such as futures contracts on pork bellies, must be traded on
public exchanges and are subject to government oversight and
regulation. The esoteric inside knowledge, on the contrary,
holds that over-the-counter derivatives, contracts that are
made directly between two parties (and thus were, according
to Wendy Gramm's edict, free of government oversight) are
an excellent medium of speculation.

As we have learned over the course of our recent troubles,

many of the firms that buy the new and improved derivatives contracts don't even have an underlying stake in the assets on which they are based. It is possible to buy naked credit default swaps to hedge against bonds that you don't even own. As a host of critics have pointed out, that is essentially the same as taking out an insurance policy on your neighbor's life. Once they were invented, these derivatives contracts, precisely because they are so risky, quickly became the profit centers of the large banks. To protect this lucrative business, a powerful lobby was formed, the International Swaps and Derivatives Association (ISDA), and that lobby pushed very hard to keep regulators out of the business. The December 2000 law, which somewhat ironically also reauthorized the expiring Commodity Futures Trading Commission, fully enshrined the questionable decisions of regulators like Wendy Gramm (who, immediately after her 1993 gift, was rewarded with a seat on Enron's board of directors, just as Robert Rubin was rewarded for his loyal service to the banks with a cochairmanship of Citigroup, a prime beneficiary of the Glass-Steagall repeal) and gave a broad legal exemption to many derivatives.

In testimony on April 8, 2010, before the Financial Crisis Inquiry Commission, a modest show trial designed to give the Obama administration some much-needed political cover, Robert Rubin was asked by commissioner Brooksley Born whether he now favored regulating derivatives. This was a wonderful moment, a moment many observers had been awaiting for months. Born had been the chairman of the Commodity Futures Trading Commission from 1996 to 1999 and had attempted to bring the derivative dark markets under the supervision and regulation of her agency, because she was convinced that they would eventually cause an economic catastrophe. Rubin, Summers, and Alan Greenspan had all attempted to shut her down and shut her up. She fought back and continued to advocate publicly for regulation. In a famous incident in 1998 Summers even called her up on the telephone and said, "I have thirteen bankers in my office and they say if you go forward with this you will cause the worst financial crisis since World War II." It wasn't long before Born was forced out. The pregnant exchange between her and Rubin in 2010 is worth quoting:

> BORN: Do you now think that there is a need for any regulation of the OTC derivatives market?
>
> RUBIN: I think that there should be, and I thought this when I was at Goldman Sachs. I think that there should be regulation of over-the-counter derivatives, but I also think that the regulation of listed derivatives should be enhanced, particularly through increased capital and margin requirements. . . .
>
> BORN: You've said in the past that there was no political will to regulate over-the-counter derivatives. In your view, was the lack of political will related to pressure by the financial services industry?
>
> RUBIN: I think there were very strongly held views in the financial services industry in opposition to regu-

lation, and I think that they were not overcomeable. That's probably not a word, overcomeable, but not surmountable at that point. . . .

BORN: Do you think that the lack of political will may also have been affected by a pervasive view that the market was appropriately self-regulatory, and that there wasn't a need for regulation?

RUBIN: I don't—that's a level of sophistication—it's a terrifically interesting and important question, but I don't think when you got into the political arena that really was what this was about. I think this was more about the interests of those who were involved and their ability to effect those interests. Effect, e-f-f, effect those interests. Rather than the much more sophisticated question that you're raising.

Rubin, forced to praise and kowtow before this woman ("it's a terrifically interesting and important question") whose regulatory career he had helped destroy, now claims he had long favored the regulation of derivatives, and so he wrote in his 2003 memoir—*In an Uncertain World: Tough Choices from Wall Street to Washington*—and yet he repeatedly intervened to prevent such regulation. Assuming he is telling the truth, and perhaps he is, Rubin gives a very revealing answer. The finance industry was not willing to be regulated, and its resistance was "not overcomeable." Why not? In his book Rubin even wrote, "While economically useful under most circumstances for more precise risk management, derivatives can pose risks when market conditions become very volatile. That occurs because of various technical factors that can cause derivatives users to suddenly need to buy or sell in the underlying markets to maintain appropriate hedge positions. With the truly vast increase in the amount of derivatives outstanding, it is at least conceivable that the effect on already disrupted markets could be vast." Why, then, was it the case that the Clinton administration, even if the secretary of the Treasury agreed with the chairman of the CFTC, was not able to regulate a systemically dangerous Wall Street practice? Because, he agrees, there was no "political will." Rubin, his large hands gesturing helplessly as he hunched before the microphone, appeared contrite and chastened. He should have been. Shortly after this testimony, Bill Clinton, who has always been very good at apologizing, came out and apologized for the CFMA. He said that Rubin and Summers had given him bad advice about the derivatives legislation—though a former aide later blamed the advice on Alan Greenspan, whose amazing transformation from financial god-king to world-historical goat-boy is worthy of Ovid's *Metamorphoses*.

BORN RESIGNED IN 1999. In 2000, Congress passed the Commodity Futures Modernization Act, which specifically exempted over-the-counter derivatives from regulation. That was a Republican congress, but in contrast to the impression that Rubin is at such pains to give, it seems that *all the political will* was solidly behind CFMA. The Clinton administration strongly supported the bill in a statement of policy issued on October 19, 2000:

> The Administration strongly supports the version of H.R. 4541, the Commodity Futures Modernization Act of 2000 . . . It is important that this legislation be enacted this year because of the meaningful steps it would take in helping to: promote innovation; enhance the transparency and efficiency of derivative markets; maintain the competitiveness of U.S. businesses and markets; and, potentially, reduce systemic risk. H.R. 4541 would accomplish these goals while assuring adequate customer protection for small investors and protecting the integrity of the underlying securities and futures markets. A failure to modernize the Nation's framework for OTC derivatives during this legislative session would deprive American markets and businesses of these important benefits and could result in the movement of these markets to overseas locations with more updated regulatory regimes.

In November, Lawrence Summers plugged the CFMA in a speech before the Securities Industry Association, and he said that the administration was "actively promoting the bill." Then, on December 14, Summers issued a press release applauding the compromise reached with Gramm over the bill's language: "We are pleased with the agreement reached last night on over-the-counter derivatives. We hope that Congress will now pass this important legislation that will allow the United States *to maintain its competitive position* in this rapidly growing sector by providing legal certainty and promoting innovation, transparency and efficiency in our financial markets." And so it came to be. America's competitive— which is to say, dominant—position in the derivatives industry was saved, and before long Enron showed the world what could be done with these dangerous instruments.

As it happens, the Enron debacle was merely a preview of what was to come—a bit of foreplay, if you will. Capitalism was definitely not standing still. Notice the italicized words in the last quotation. Any and everything that policy makers do can be rationalized in terms of maintaining America's "competitive position." But note the position in which these decisions place the American public: all too often, we're bent over a chair. Corporate America likes to be on top.

Despite the long list of political and economic atrocities attributable to their legacy, Senator Barack Obama was full of praise for what Reagan and his acolyte Bill Clinton wrought. Yet he knew that people weren't happy with what was going on in America under the reign of George W. Bush. He clearly knew that he had to promise something big and beautiful and audacious. Strangely, however, despite the rhetorical buildup and the swelling orchestration, all he ever seemed to come up with was that boring model of communicative rationality known as *consensus*. We've seen how enamored of bipartisanship he is, and his most consistent promise has been to heal the nasty divide in Washington and in the heartland, to bring people together, *e pluribus unum*. In *The Audacity of Hope* he offers up the inspiring example of Abraham Lincoln and boils down the "simple maxim" of that great maker of rhetoric to a sparkling banality: "we should be guided by what works."

Then, after a swift enumeration of the usual nostrums such as education and "critical" investments in high technology and biofuels and after much back-and-forth, comparing of hands, and putting down of liberals and labor unions—asserting, for instance, that many on the left believe that "more spending alone will improve educational outcomes"—he lands on trade. The careful reader will by now know what to expect; although Obama, as a Democrat, naturally supports "not just free trade but fair trade," effective labor protections, better environmental regulations, the prohibition of child labor and of currency manipulation, and better copyright and patent protections, he knows that the "underlying realities of globalization" will remain. That's right: more relentless advances and pools. But of course, like the good derivatives trader that he is, dealing in insolvent tranches of bankrupt ideas and empty phrases, Obama won't unambiguously reveal his true position. "The conventional wisdom," he writes, as if distancing himself from what will follow, "among policy makers, the press, and the business community these days is that free trade makes everyone better off." For every job that disappears owing to offshoring and layoffs, "so the argument goes," another one or more than one will be created by "expanding service sectors." So the argument goes, he says, in what might be called a misdirection play, analogous to taking an option position directly opposed to your true stake in a particular market. If you weren't careful you might think Obama was about to launch into a counterargument that would demolish this conventional wisdom about "free" trade. Instead, in a rhetorical feint, he acknowledges the worries of those who are troubled by the results of globalization so far, and points to evidence, were he to develop the argument, that would show the conventional wisdom to be quite simply a lie, before retreating into some decidedly fuzzy logic. He's troubled, he feels our pain, and he wonders what to do. He understands why "some might want to put a stop to globalization—to freeze the status quo and insulate ourselves from economic disruption." Here, then, appears Robert Rubin, the deus ex machina, to explain away the paradoxes and contradictions of monopoly capitalism and justify the ways of Obama to men.

While he was "on a stop" in New York, Obama writes, he just happened to mention to Robert Rubin some of the studies of economic disruptions he'd been reading. He doesn't tell us what he was doing in New York, but we can be reasonably sure he was raising money. He had met Rubin during his campaign for the Senate, he tells us, and he acknowledges that "it would be hard to find a Democrat more closely identified with globalization than Rubin—not only had he been one of Wall Street's most influential bankers for decades, but for much of the nineties he had helped chart the course of world finance." That, I submit, is the most unambiguously accurate statement in his entire chapter. Obama continues, "He also happens to be one of the more thoughtful and unassuming people I know." It would be hard to find an example of higher praise in Obama's literary oeuvre. And he then quotes Rubin at length as the wise banker, in a very Obama-like fashion, cautiously, oh so cautiously argues that the "economists are probably right" to say that there's no "inherent limit to the number of new jobs" the American economy can generate. We are an ingenious people, he was suggesting. We invent new industries, new wants, new needs. Look at American history and the manifold examples of our innovation and enterprise. Yet like any well-trained financial adviser, Rubin carefully hedged his predictions: "Of course, there's no guarantee that the pattern holds this time." Caveat emptor: past performance is no guarantee of future returns! Just look at any securities contract, read the fine print on your mutual fund agreement or your e-trade account. Never forget that Rubin is a former chairman of Goldman Sachs, a company that specializes in ripping the face off its customers.

Obama hazards that the good folks in Galesburg, buffeted by the strong winds of globalized finance, might not be so reassured by Rubin's outlook. "I said it's possible, not probable." Oh, right. "I tend to be cautiously optimistic that if we get our fiscal house in order and improve our educational system, their children will do just fine. Anyway, there's one thing that I would tell the people in Galesburg *is* certain. Any efforts at protectionism will be counterproductive—and it will make their children worse off in the bargain." The sage had spoken: he's "cautiously optimistic" that if the American people will continue to follow his economic recipe, all will be well. The irony is almost too much to bear. Obliviously, unaware of the disaster to come, Obama hangs on these clichés and empty phrases as if they were uttered by the Sibyl herself. He was happy to hear that Rubin could also feel the pain of those unemployed Maytag workers, that he could acknowledge that they "had legitimate cause for concern"; and, by the way— because he can't help himself, he always has to keep things balanced and centrist—most labor leaders, in his experience, aren't "kneejerk protectionists," but are, in fact, deep thinkers on this subject.

And, finally, the punch line: "Still, it was hard to deny Rubin's basic insight: We can try to slow globalization, but we can't stop it." Take that, you pools and advances!

From that "basic insight," which happens to be perfectly consistent with Obama's version of Hamilton's and Lincoln's "basic insight," which is more or less the same as Reagan's "central insight," it all follows. We will tinker along the edges, but globalization—by which Rubin means, make no mistake, deregulated international capital flows above all, not merely the byzantine system of trade rules that encourage American corporations to exploit low labor costs and nonexistent environmental policies in poor countries—is bigger and more powerful than any old-fashioned vision of democracy or republican government. The task, as Obama sees it, is thus to "distribute the costs and the benefits of globalization more fairly across the population." And that, he makes clear, means recasting the crumbling social compact of the New Deal for the needs of the twenty-first century. He mentions tax credits, flexible education accounts, wage insurance, and nudgy little initiatives like creating opt-out 401(k) plans so that employees will automatically be enrolled unless they specify otherwise. He endorses Paygo, a Clinton-era law requiring that all new expenditures be balanced with spending cuts. Obama also consults another capitalist sage, Warren Buffett, whom he quotes at length in a declaration that rich people ought to pay slightly higher taxes. Obama says that labor rights should be shored up, and he goes on about health-care reform and asserts, ominously, that we have to "preserve Social Security's essential character and shore up its solvency." Rich people, Obama continues, can afford to pay slightly more, and they have no reason to complain about the way they've been treated in the American system—nor, he makes clear, do they have anything to fear from Barack Obama. Those who have eyes to see—and no one has sharper eyes than America's top earners—have witnessed the testimony of Warren Buffett and, above all, Robert Rubin, and they can rest assured that their American Dream will not be taken away, even if it is a nightmare for the rest of us.

Thus ends the lesson, with an evocation of Jefferson and the dissonant admission, included to make sure his big misdirection play has been successful, that the author of the Declaration of Independence did in fact have good reason to fear the Hamiltonian system, and he reminds us once again that the power of money in our system is a bad thing, that we don't have enough "countervailing voices to remind us of who we are and where we've come from, and to affirm our bond with one another." And like the good sophist that he unquestionably is, Obama returns to his elegant frame, the private jets, and his decision to impose a ban on using them. Instead, he would put up with the hassle of commercial flights and with waiting in lines. But as it happens, on a commercial plane he met a man who had Parkinson's disease, and got to hear about this man's challenges and his hopes and his dreams and his fervent wish that Congress would do something about stem-cell research. "These are the moments you miss," Obama thought to himself, "when you fly on a private jet."

CHAPTER FOUR

BUYER BEWARE

When it came time for the president-elect to pick his economic team, as we know, he decided upon *continuity* rather than *change*, selecting as his secretary of the Treasury Timothy Geithner, the president of the Federal Reserve Bank of New York, the regulator with direct responsibility for the banks whose insolvency created the financial crisis, and one of the primary architects of President Bush's disastrous initial bank bailout, known as the Troubled Assets Relief Program (TARP). Obama apparently decided that Lawrence Summers, whose tenure as president of Harvard was perhaps too controversial for his tastes, was better suited for a somewhat less visible post as director of the National Economic Council, an office occupied by Rubin before he became Treasury secretary. In that position Summers immediately went to work to solidify his power base, duly marginalizing Paul Volcker, who had advised Obama during the campaign and helped write his best-received economic speech. Volcker, everyone knew from his record as Fed chairman in the 1970s, would be unlikely to appease the banks or cover up the failings of regulators, so it was important for Summers to neutralize him. Summers, who was among the chief architects of the failed deregulatory policies that helped create the financial crisis, had a direct personal interest in trying to prove that his policies were not at fault.

In other words, despite his vaunted pragmatism and his determination to be "guided by what works," Obama chose as his two closest economic advisers men whose understanding of the failed policies of the past could hardly be more intimate—precisely because they bear direct personal responsibility for those policies and thus for the ensuing crisis, which not only destroyed trillions of dollars in fictitious wealth but has also inflicted untold miseries on millions of Americans, who have lost their jobs and their homes and have little prospect of ever recovering their vanished standard of living. Ben Bernanke, the chairman of the Federal Reserve and the third man in Obama's economic triumvirate, can be seen as an added catastrophic bonus, since his term was not due to expire until 2010. With the possible exception of Geithner, Bernanke was the second-worst bank regulator in America— the first rank belonging, without question, to Alan Greenspan, who carefully nurtured one economic bubble after another during his long tenure at the Fed.

To be sure, Obama was stepping into the middle of an extraordinary situation, but he also had time to come to grips with what was going on. The housing bubble had finally begun its messy collapse in August 2007, when banks suddenly came to the realization that they no longer trusted one another and interest rates on short-term intra-bank loans suddenly shot up. Since credit, as the word itself implies, is founded on trust, the credit markets seized up, and in playgrounds across New York City—I remember it well because I was at the time trying and failing to get a mortgage commitment letter from Wells Fargo!—worried parents began murmuring about an economic catastrophe. Residential mortgages, which for years had been ripe for the plucking, were suddenly scarce. Without the influx of new mortgages, the banks' speculative engines began to run out of fuel, and despite their best efforts, Bernanke and Treasury Secretary Henry Paulson were unable to keep the bubble inflated with interest rate cuts and the purchasing power of Fannie Mae and Freddie Mac, an unsuccessful shadow bailout that was apparently meant to avoid the embarrassment of going to Congress for help in the middle of a presidential election. Significantly, the Federal Reserve also set up a special lending facility to extend short-term credit to the troubled banks, a device that permitted such loans to be carried out in secret, in contrast to loans made through the Fed's discount window. This single-payer insurance plan for Wall Street was justified by the claim that the markets would punish banks if it was known which ones were taking emergency loans; as perceptive observers pointed out, this decision was especially ironic, since it was a tacit admission that our market fundamentalist central bankers, when it comes down to it, do not trust the invisible hand of the market to do what is right and necessary.

Paulson and the Fed soon astonished the world by arranging for the purchase of Bear Stearns by JPMorgan Chase and agreeing to guarantee $30 billion worth of toxic assets. The Fed also offered other investment banks the same low-interest credit that commercial banks enjoy, though without the regulatory scrutiny and restrictions that normally go along with that security. Fannie Mae and Freddie Mac then faced collapse and were eventually taken over by federal authorities. Then, notoriously, Bernanke, Geithner, and Paulson permitted Lehman Brothers simply to implode, and its bankruptcy fully exposed the fragility of the world's financial system. Days after letting Lehman fail, they decided to nationalize AIG, taking 80 percent ownership and passing tens of billions through the company to rescue firms such as Goldman Sachs, who had purchased credit default swaps from the giant insurance company. Bush's triumvirate then went to Congress and demanded unlimited and unsupervised power—justified, they said, to prevent a new Great Depression—in a three-page authorization that Congress rightly rejected. After a brief hurly-burly of hysteria stoked by the media, a revised plan to purchase toxic assets was passed by Congress, over the massive objections of the general public, whereupon Bush's three blind mice decided to do something else entirely. Instead of buying toxic assets, the government would inject capital into the banks in return for equity.

We all know what happened next: an almost unlimited

rolling federal bailout of the financial industry, with the government's exposure reaching, by conservative estimates, $12 trillion. That sum includes the original $700 billion allocated for the comically euphemistic Troubled Assets Relief Program—not all of which was spent and much of which was paid back (though without any compensation to the public for the risk it took on by advancing those low-interest and no-interest loans) as banks sought to avoid government restrictions on executive compensation—as well as a dizzying number of additional programs and emergency measures, including the bailout of Bear Sterns, the rescue of AIG, the takeover of Washington Mutual, the Bank of America loan-loss backstop, the Citigroup loan-loss backstop, purchases of mortgaged-backed securities from Fannie Mae and Freddie Mac, the Public Private Partnership Investment Program, the bailouts of the automakers, and Obama's stimulus package. In July 2009, Neil Barofsky, the inspector general for the bailout programs, estimated in testimony before Congress that the bailouts could eventually cost $23.7 trillion, though he did say that this figure was a worst-case scenario. It was immediately pointed out in the press that $23 trillion is greater than the combined cost of all the wars the United States has ever fought. World War II, for example, came in at $4.1 trillion, adjusted for inflation, and the New Deal cost a mere $500 billion. Accounting for how much money has actually been spent is an almost impossible task because no one knows how much the Federal Reserve has really been spending since it has usurped Congress's appropriation power and has successfully resisted calls for a thorough audit.

The Bush administration and the Obama administration each seemed to be concerned above all else with making sure that the banking community and Wall Street in general were satisfied with its efforts. Certainly the rest of the citizenry was not. Joseph Stiglitz has characterized the bank bailouts as "among the most costly mistakes of any government at any time." In short, as Stiglitz and many other economists have argued, both Bush and Obama did everything wrong. Long-established procedures would have involved taking over the big banks, examining their books, and resolving them by selling off their assets, just as the FDIC does routinely with smaller institutions. But the Obama administration, following the advice of Timothy Geithner, instead declared that these banks were too big to fail and then rewarded the people who had caused the crisis, thereby increasing moral hazard and the likelihood of further irresponsible behavior. The administration wasted trillions of dollars without addressing the underlying instabilities; it failed to demand control of the banks that it had essentially purchased; and it failed to exact significant concessions in exchange for government aid. TARP participants were asked to fill out a simple two-page form, several orders of magnitude less complex and less onerous than an application for unemployment insurance or food stamps.

Bush's mishandling of the crisis was typical; he first denied that there was a crisis, then demanded limitless power to meet it. It would have been shocking if he had done anything different. Obama's, however, was unforgivable. Not only did he squander his own credibility, but he damaged for the foreseeable future the cause of liberal government by seemingly demonstrating, as if in a deliberate reductio ad absurdum, that government cannot be trusted to intervene in the economy, thereby giving credence to the nostalgic barking of naive economic libertarians. As much as we might wish to live in a society simple enough to do without a regulatory state, that horse has been out of the barn for centuries. The so-called free-market is a figment of the modern imagination, a phantasm, a mirage. Not even Thomas Jefferson fully subscribed to the laissez-faire gospel, and no contemporary republican politics should allow itself to be distracted by those old dogmas.

The fundamental error of economic libertarians is one of faith, faith in the divine efficiency of the almighty market. And, like chiliastic Christians everywhere, market fundamentalists—no matter how many times events refute their articles of faith—can be relied upon to find some handy explanation, usually involving bureaucratic malfeasance, for avoiding the plain fact that any market more complex than a vegetable cart requires regulation. Market fundamentalists believe that if government would simply get out of the way, the goodness and virtue of our enlightened businessmen would lead us to a promised land of milk and honey and gold-plated bathroom fixtures. They would be better off attending to the hard teachings of Machiavelli, who observed that "it is necessary for him who lays out a state and arranges laws for it to presuppose that all men are evil and that they are always going to act according to the wickedness of their spirits whenever they have free scope." This is a fine maxim for business regulation and one well borne out by the housing bubble, as is its corollary: "Men never do anything good except by necessity."

It's hard to imagine a less regulated market than the OTC

derivatives market. Under no possible reconstruction of the facts can government bureaucrats be blamed for causing the meltdown through overzealous regulation. Not only did that market not work; its failure almost brought down the whole infrastructure of world finance. This was not simply a matter of the banks' getting in over their heads, a failure to follow prudent leverage and margin guidelines. As former bank regulators such as William Black have tirelessly pointed out since the debacle began, old-fashioned accounting-control fraud certainly played a large role as well. The signs of fraud are everywhere, despite the paucity of criminal investigations to date. Liar loans (stated income) and NINJA loans (no income, no job, no assets) were premised on fraud. Lehman Brothers, like Enron before it, used accounting gimmicks to hide its liabilities not only from regulators but from the markets, and there is every indication that many other Wall Street firms were using similar tactics. In April it was reported that eighteen large banks, including Goldman Sachs, Morgan Stanley, JPMorgan Chase, Bank of America, and Citigroup, had been lowering their debt by an average of 42 percent at each of the previous five quarters. Such accounting tricks may or may not be legal, but they create a misleading picture of an institution's health.

The entertaining civil fraud case filed by the Securities and Exchange Commission against Goldman Sachs for devising a synthetic derivative product—the now famous Abacus 2007 AC1 transaction—so that a large hedge fund run by John Paulson could bet against the housing market is another sign of the strange fruit investors have harvested from financial deregulation. It's clear that many other firms were engaged in the same practices, and there is strong evidence that short bets on the subprime market drove demand for more junk mortgages and helped inflate the bubble, thus significantly increasing the damage caused by its collapse. The positive response to the Goldman probe appears to have emboldened the usually timid SEC to examine other such deals; those underpaid regulators could spend their lives at the task.

Criminal investigators, both federal and state, are also said to be looking into the activities of Goldman and other financial companies, but given Goldman's prominent stake in the Democratic Party, it would be surprising if even the most hated firm on Wall Street were seriously damaged by the suit, especially if the other banks are sued as well. It's difficult to believe that the federal government would destroy all the largest banks with criminal fraud convictions after spending trillions to keep them in business; unfortunately, "too big to fail" in all likelihood means "too big to be convicted." Yet even if the bankers were to be so severely chastened that they withdrew from politics in a fit of pique (an utterly utopian prospect), our infinitely adaptable system of influence would soon replace them with other willing investors. The Marines may land on Wall Street, just as they did in the long-ago 1930s, but even the New Deal was unable to prevent the continued corrupt influence of America's economic royalists. A multibillion-dollar fine, some scolding from underpaid functionaries, a bit of bad press, and a few lost clients are the most likely outcome. Civil fines rarely cause enough pain to change behavior on Wall Street.

Of course, it could always happen that the civil suit will uncover evidence of unambiguous criminality, and the Obama administration may decide that the political advantages of a prosecution outweigh all the normal cynical calculations that usually prevail in these cases. It would be an unusual stroke of justice if Goldman Sachs or one of the other too-big-to-fail banks now under belated scrutiny joined the dear departed Enron on the killing floor of famous frauds, a rare demonstration that even the most powerful political investors can get burned. If that happens and their political usefulness expires, the banks will receive no mercy from their erstwhile creatures in Washington. Past performance, remember, is no guarantee of future results.

After Obama was inaugurated, financial reform legislation languished in Congress for more than a year. Although the House passed a bill in December 2009, a Senate bill was not released by Christopher Dodd until negotiations with Republicans in the Senate Finance Committee broke down during the high drama of the epic health-care battle in March. That was eighteen months after the collapse of Lehman Brothers triggered the most acute phase of the financial crisis—a crisis that began in the summer of 2007, when credit markets collapsed as the largest American banks realized they were essentially insolvent. Neither Barney Frank's House bill nor Dodd's Senate bill received particularly good reviews from critics. The financial crisis was largely a result of the insolvency of the major banks and banklike institutions—their liabilities, often in the form of mortgage-backed derivatives, far exceeded their assets. None of them were quite willing to admit this disturbing fact, not even to themselves, it seems; but neither could they deny that determining their exact risk exposure was virtually impossible, given the complexity of the fix they'd derived and speculated themselves into.

Frank's bill, despite token efforts, effectively authorized current practices and included enough loopholes and blind spots to ensure that many over-the-counter derivatives would remain unregulated. Dodd's initial bill was thought to be slightly better, but instead of a freestanding Consumer Financial Protection Agency, as in the House bill, it safely tucked the watchdog agency into the Federal Reserve, which historically has been subservient to bankers and operates under a mandate to preserve the health and solvency of banks, not individual households. The bill as written also gave the Federal Reserve control over the new agency's budget, so it would have the power to weaken the consumer agency at will, and even the Fed's budget is outside the control of Congress. Tellingly, the derivatives section of the bill, which goes to the heart of the matter, was at first a mere placeholder, awaiting the outcome of further negotiations.

Congress's reluctance to take on derivatives was understandable, considering the hold that the finance industry has on the lawmakers who populate the controlling committees, though given the size of the threat posed by this market it is quite literally insane. Chris Dodd, for instance, received more than \$15 million from the FIRE sector from 1989 to 2009, and the money continued to pour in during the 2010 cycle even after he announced his retirement. His largest contributors include Citigroup, Bear Stearns, Goldman Sachs, Morgan Stanley, General Electric, JPMorgan Chase, and Merrill Lynch. His decision to retire surely had nothing to do with the revelation, in the midst of the Countrywide Financial scandal, that he had received below-market loans from his good friend Angelo Mozilo, the company's CEO. Frank, a somewhat less amiable figure who specializes in denouncing his backers even as he protects their interests with masterful behind-the-scenes maneuvering, received $3,158,160 from the FIRE sector between 1989 and 2009; his top contributor during that period was the American Bankers Association, followed closely by JPMorgan Chase and National Association of Realtors.

The Bank for International Settlements estimates that the OTC derivatives market currently has a notional value of more than $600 trillion; according to Gary Gensler, the chairman of the Commodity Futures Trading Commission, the notional value of such contracts in the United States alone is $300 trillion, almost twenty times the size of the real American economy. Much of this market is controlled by the big banks, and despite all the bellowing about hedging risk and providing liquidity, it is increasingly clear that a very large fraction of these contracts are unproductive and speculative. For a few million dollars, invested over decades with powerful lawmakers, the finance industry manages to protect a fragile, ill-defined, and unregulated market that casts a long and ominous speculative shadow over the real economy.

In his January 2010 quarterly report to Congress on the TARP program, Neil Barofsky summed up the lack of progress on financial reform in unambiguous terms: "The substantial costs of TARP—in money, moral hazard effects on the market, and Government credibility—will have been for naught if we do nothing to correct the fundamental problems in our financial system and end up in a similar or even greater crisis in two, or five, or ten years' time. It is hard to see how any of the fundamental problems in the system have been addressed to date." Barofsky proceeded to point out that the enormous too-big-to-fail institutions, not only banks but shadow banking entities like AIG, not only are still in existence but have grown even larger and more systemically dangerous; that the "heads, I win—tails the government will bail me out" approach to finance has been reenforced by the Obama administration's blank check to the banks; that the extension of the TARP program until October 3, 2010, reinforces the perception among the systemically dangerous institutions that the government remains committed to the too-big-to-fail policy; that Wall Street's culture of excessive compensation remains filled with perverse incentives; and that the Obama administration's attempts to support housing prices risk reinflating the housing bubble. "Stated another way," Barofsky wrote, "even if TARP saved our financial system from driving off a cliff back in 2008, absent meaningful reform, we are still driving on the same winding mountain road, but this time in a faster car."

Despite the token public scoldings, the Obama administration has consistently supported a class of banks and shadow banks that are no longer obliged to abide by the normal rules of capitalism, such as they are. Currently, the largest six U.S. banks control assets greater than 63 percent of GDP; fifteen years ago, those banks controlled assets valued at only 17 percent of GDP. Joseph Stiglitz does not shy away from the obvious: "All of this discussion about too-big-to-fail banks was just a ruse. It was a ploy that worked, based on fearmongering. Just as Bush used 9/11 and the fears of terrorism to justify so much of what he did, the Treasury under both Bush and Obama used 9/15—the day that Lehman collapsed—and the fears of another meltdown as a tool to extract as much as possible for the banks and the bankers that had brought the world to the brink of economic ruin." Not only do such banks distort the capital markets, but their growth prevents smaller banks from thriving, and the enormous outlay of government funding squanders resources that would be better spent elsewhere— on health care, jobs, alternative energy, infrastructure, and restructuring the mortgages of distressed homeowners. The big banks, including the investment banks that now enjoy the status of commercial banks and thus the full faith and credit of the United States, serve no productive social purpose; they are not even really banks anymore, since most of their profits come from trading and speculation. These large corporations have thus not only distorted the financial system but fundamentally warped the political system as well.

How this has come about is not exactly a mystery. In addition to campaign contributions, the financial sector spent more than $467 million on lobbying in 2009, and that is out of a record total of $3.47 billion spent lobbying the federal government. The only sectors that spent more than finance were health at almost $545 million, and miscellaneous business at more than $567 million, and that includes the U.S. Chamber of Commerce, which spent $144 million all by itself. Naturally, there is much overlap here, and since various reform proposals and stimulus packages were in the works, big business was particularly keen to get its way that year. During the first quarter of 2010, lobbying was even more extreme: $903 million was spent by March 31, about $19 million a day. Despite the pathetic bleating of thin-skinned Wall Street multimillionaires that Obama is being mean to them, and the threats that corporate contributions would dry up, almost half the political money from the financial sector and from business in general was still flowing into the accounts of Democrats: 43 percent of investments by the FIRE sector and 46 percent of business contributions overall. That's a significant drop from last year's take, and it is clearly a warning to Democrats not to go too far with finance reform—but despite Wall Street's evident hurt feelings it can also be seen less as a repudiation of the Democrats than as a market signal. Many political investors suspect that the Republicans will make large gains in the midterms, so they are hedging their stake in the Democrats by diversifying their political portfolios. Once the finance bill passes into law, Democrats like errant lovers will no doubt seek to make up with their estranged suitors. Nothing will change. The root problem is the political power of the large banks and banklike institutions. Until their power is broken, no real reform of our financial system can possibly take hold.

The stock market panic of May 6 that took place as lawmakers dickered over amendments, loopholes, and carve-outs for this or that financial subinterest pointed to the inadequacy of the measures being considered. As compelling as they were, questions over whether to audit the Fed, break up the too-big-to-fail banks, force the sale of derivative businesses, impose a ban on proprietary trading, set up a bailout mechanism to be funded by a tax on banks, or require living wills in the case of collapse all had precisely no relevance to the black swan that suddenly flew over Wall Street, causing the Dow to drop 1,000 points and $1 trillion to vanish in minutes as the value of major stocks dropped to zero, before recovering just as rapidly. Bankers' long-standing influence in Congress combined with the Obama administration's steady pressure against any truly substantive reforms guaranteed that none of the stronger proposals being debated in the Senate had a prayer of becoming law anyway. For example, the Brown-Kaufman SAFE Banking Act, which would have limited the size and leverage of the largest banks, was opposed by the White House as well as by powerful senators such as Dodd and Charles Schumer, who has collected even more FIRE money ($15,856,041) than Dodd over the last twenty years; Schumer's top donor is Goldman Sachs. It failed 61-33, with the Democrats voting against it 30-27. The compromise Sanders amendment on auditing the Fed and ending its long tradition of unaccountability passed unanimously after it was reduced under pressure from the administration to a very limited onetime release of the names of banks that had engaged in emergency borrowing since December 1, 2007. Nothing with any teeth could possibly pass 96-0. A ludicrous drift net of regulations was being fashioned just as automatic trading programs no one can control nearly crashed the American stock markets for reasons no one fully understand; and our wise lawmakers—with notable exceptions like Senator Ted

Kaufman, who warned of the dangers of trading programs back in September 2009—just continued to debate modest tinkerings that will do little to prevent the next crisis.

Why not? Because there is no *political will*—meaning, of course, that the powerful interests who have the largest stakes in the system as it exists are unwilling to accept regulation that forces them to alter their behavior fundamentally, in a situation where nothing short of fundamental reform will do. The elements of such reform, as many able economists have argued, are actually fairly simple: force the banks and the pseudo banks to downsize by removing government protection and enforcing market discipline; limit deposit insurance to keep institutions from growing too big and too fast; enforce strict and conservative leverage limits; bring the derivatives markets in out of the shadows and force banks to hold their loans until maturity; reimpose the Glass-Steagall fire wall between investment and commercial banking; forbid banks to hold derivatives or to engage in proprietary trading; impose a transaction tax to limit high-frequency trading; and use direct government lending to encourage socially desirable ends where markets are not viable. Banks would necessarily become relatively small and dull again, the source of modest profits and abundant golf time for bankers, and socially and economically valuable credit for the larger community. The common theme of the best proposals is that we must abolish a system that ruthlessly socializes risk and market downside while privatizing all profit and upside. Although the reform bills contain some decent provisions, no one should be under any illusions: the banks have triumphed once again.

The danger of a new crisis can hardly be exaggerated; days after the mysterious flash crash the European Union announced a $957 billion rescue package in response to the debt crisis faced by Greece and other vulnerable EU economies. President Obama had even made anxious phone calls urging decisive action to restore confidence to the markets. And so a mighty financial spell was cast, though market soothsayers and medicine men expressed due skepticism that even so large a conjuration would suffice to calm the animal spirits of a system that has grown too large and complex and interrelated for even a confederacy of finance ministers drawn from the world's largest and most powerful states to comprehend and manage. No one even pretends that the American financial reform law, when it finally passes, will suffice to protect us from the contagion of another credit crisis, especially since the usual historical sequence according to which reform typically *follows* congressional and criminal investigations has been decisively inverted by the Obama regime. We are left, then, with large financial firms that are unwilling to submit to a reduction in profits in exchange for broad security. Meanwhile, the lawmakers who depend on them are unwilling and unable to do what is necessary to protect society from their depredations. Those of us who pretend to eighteenth-century citizenship, to the citizenship of flesh-and-blood human beings who wield ballots as the tokens of our interests, should heed these unmistakable signs and portents. Our political will has no influence.

CHAPTER FIVE

MONSTERS OF SEDITION

Principles, in politics as in logic, define one's field of possibilities. In politics and civil life our principles of thought and action are historical. Although revolutions overtake political regimes, disrupting societies and promising radical change, they rarely succeed in breaking free from the traditions that previously supported and constrained individuals in their striving for power and recognition. So it is with us in the United States. Although our language has drifted and our historical attention span has collapsed, many of the fundamental antagonisms that emerged immediately after the American Revolution remain very much in play. Conflicts over credit and banking lie at the heart of our constitutional politics and at the origin of our party system, which in many ways functions as an unwritten or shadow constitution that subverts the clear meaning of our official written founding charter. The source of such conflicts is the tendency of credit and financial innovation to introduce instabilities into the system of property and thus into the balance of power in the state. As republicans have long understood, control of credit amounts to control over the distribution of wealth.

The ideological origins of the American Revolution can be found in the modern republican commonwealth tradition of radical Whig pamphleteers and polemicists who raged against the excesses of British ministerial administration in the eighteenth century. In addition to the political tracts of John Locke, whose name generations of American schoolchildren were once taught to spell, Americans in the eighteenth century were reading the polemics of the English Country party, which largely took its inspiration from the great Roman historians and orators, Machiavelli and other Italian Renaissance republicans, and the radical republicans of the English Civil War such as James Harrington, John Milton, and Algernon Sidney. John Trenchard and Thomas Gordon, writing under the pseudonym Cato, in the 1720s published a series of essays in the *London Journal* that became one of the canonical expressions of the radical Whigs; those essays were republished in the American colonies and became one of the primary vehicles of republican ideas, inspiring countless revolutionary and postrevolutionary polemics among both the advocates of the Constitution and the anti-federalists who opposed it.

What animated these republican authors above all was the menace of corruption, a broad political concept whose meanings ranged from common bribery and embezzlement or any mercenary subversion of public office to the rich metaphor of a spreading cancer attacking the vital organs of the body politic. Social change, moral depravity, instability, and the dissolution of a government into a more illiberal or repressive regime were all contained in the notion. Civil corruption might come about for any number of reasons, but the consistent fear of the Country tradition was the corrupting influence of executive power, which through the patronage of offices, an immortal national debt, and the Bank of England had destroyed the independence of Parliament and had thus encroached on the people's liberty. These corrupting engines of government were seen as infernal machines for the enhancement of the English crown's wealth and war-making power.

Banks, trading companies, speculation in stocks, and other commercial innovations were particularly suspect, because they created unprecedented wealth among a class of men who displayed no loyalty to the commonwealth. As Trenchard and Gordon put it, "Very great riches in private men are always dangerous to states, because they create greater dependence than can be consistent with the security of any sort of government whatsoever; they . . . destroy, among the Commons, that balance of property and power, which is necessary to a democracy, or the democratic part of any government, overthrow the poise of it, and indeed alter its nature, though not its name." Such mobile property, as opposed to fixed and real property in land, was an object of suspicion, not least because it was easily transferred across national borders. But it was the rise of *public* credit combined with modern finance that was particularly worrisome, because it created a novel and complex means for speculators to profit out of the public purse. Such government by money greatly increased the state's war-making powers, led to an increase of taxes to service the debt, and gave rise to speculative schemes that ensnared honest people and caused their ruin. This new type of credit, Trenchard and Gordon wrote, had delivered the people into the "ravenous and polluted jaws of vultures and tigers," sacrificing the property of thousands "to satiate the gluttony of a few." "This has inverted the economy and policy of nations; made a great kingdom turn all gamesters; and men have acquired the reputation of wisdom, from their skill in picking pockets." Government had been subverted as well, as if its proper role "was not to protect people in their property, but to cheat them out of it . . . by enabling artful men to circumvent the unwary; by stamping the public seal upon counterfeit wares; or by constantly coining a new sort of property, of a precarious, uncertain, and transitory value."

The great danger of this corrupting form of credit was the subversion of balanced government and its tendency to introduce dependency upon moneyed interests. In republican theory, dependency was the great evil, for any person who was dependent on another's arbitrary will was by definition a slave. Liberty was understood primarily in these terms: not merely as the absence of interference, but as the absence of arbitrary power. And for this tradition, ownership of property was the most readily available means of achieving the independence that was the necessary foundation of liberty.

Consequently, republican theorists since Aristotle had emphasized the centrality of property and its distribution among the populace, and James Harrington, whose influence on the English republican tradition is pervasive, had put the balance of property squarely at the center of his thinking.

Harrington and his republican followers did not require that there be a perfect balance of property in the commonwealth; they required only that it not be so concentrated as to subvert the form of the government. "All government," Harrington wrote, "is interest." As long as the many, or the people, held "the whole, or two parts in three, of the whole land or territory, the interest of the many or of the people is the predominant interest," and the result is democracy. But if a few men have the whole, or two-thirds of the whole, and the interest of the few predominate, then an aristocracy results. A similar analysis holds for monarchy. If, however, contrary to the natural order of things, there is a mismatch between the balance of property and the interest that prevails in the commonwealth, if property is distributed more widely than interest, there results a *privation* of government, and tyranny, oligarchy, or anarchy results. Given such premises, it is not hard to see why republicans were predisposed to consider the government of England tyrannical. Not only was royal patronage subverting the independence of the House of Commons, but financial innovation had created a class of stockjobbers and speculators who amassed great fortunes by what seemed to be mere trickery—a transitory, precarious, and uncertain kind of property that was as likely to lose its value entirely as it was to appreciate. Those with real property, however, were certain to be taxed to pay the crown's debts, often for wars unlikely to serve the interest of the public. Given England's mishandling of colonial policy, its aggressive taxation and insistence that the colonists remain dependent and subservient, it was inevitable that the republican tradition would become a fertile source of revolutionary inspiration.

After the revolution, the diversity of the constitutions of the American states, with their popular uproars, paper-money inflation, and suspension of debts, together with other apparent weaknesses of the Articles of Confederation and Perpetual Union, created a strong movement for reform, mostly with an eye to improving the terms regulating commerce and taxation—a movement that culminated in the Philadelphia convention of the summer of 1787. In business terms, the first U.S. constitution had been a disaster. Thirteen different sovereignties pursuing thirteen different policies, with different duties and taxes, made interstate commerce exceedingly complicated. "New Jersey, placed between Philadelphia and New York," wrote James Madison, "was likened to a cask tapped at both ends; and North Carolina, between Virginia and South Carolina, to a patient bleeding at both arms." It was difficult for merchants in one state to collect debts from those in another, and disputes often arose regarding depreciated currency. In monetary terms, things had been bad during colonial times and they became even more complicated after the revolution, since Parliament was no longer in a position of authority and the Articles of Confederation did not impose order on the monetary system. Indeed, the first steps toward the convention were entirely commercial in nature, particularly a conference called by Virginia with the aim of recommending new measures for the regulation of trade, a proposal that led directly to the Constitutional Convention.

After the ratification of the new Constitution, much of the former animus between the advocates and opponents was temporarily set aside amid the general celebration, but it was not long before the conflict over the charter began anew, and the old republican theories were soon brought to bear upon the new government. This time, however, the force of the republican attack was aimed not at the Constitution itself but at those who were accused of attempting to subvert it and turn it toward monarchy, in spirit if not in name. Alexander Hamilton, with his innovative economic program, lit the spark that ignited the party war that has raged almost without interruption to this day, though it is nowadays a pale and insubstantial reflection of its more vigorous and principled early manifestations. Hamilton advocated a modern system of energetic government, and his initial proposals included the chartering of a national bank, the creation of a running national debt, the assumption of the revolutionary debt and state debts, and protective tariffs and other measures designed to encourage domestic manufacturing. He also laid the foundation for an aggressive foreign policy controlled, above all, by the executive. Hamilton was a careful student and admirer of England's imperial policies, which he thought were excellently designed to promote both prosperity and national greatness. Madison, who by the Second Congress was leading the emerging opposition to what Hamilton revealingly referred to as "my administration," was appalled by Hamilton's plans, which pointedly ignored agrarian interests, and did everything in his power to prevent their enactment.

It might seem odd that there is nothing in the Constitution about banks, since banks were a common subject of political controversy, as was the question of money. As it happens, banks were popular inside the convention but extremely unpopular outside it; leaving banks out of the document can be seen as a tactical maneuver, to eliminate a potential obstacle to ratification. The issue in the persistent clamor over money was philosophical as well as political: paper money was an abstraction that confounded some of the most sophisticated minds of the day; it appeared to be an object of pure fancy, a confection spun out of nothingness. Wealth founded on paper money was airy and insubstantial, utterly dependent on the opinion of others, and consequently could hardly be the basis of the independence required of a free citizen. The bills of credit and banknotes that circulated and were used as money derived their value from specie deposited in a bank and thus were structurally similar to the derivatives that are the source of so much political and financial consternation today. Then as now, the activities of banks were often highly destructive of the real economy, and the law had not yet caught up with their innovations.

Once the new government was formed—after squabbling over whether President Washington should be addressed as "Your Highness," "Your Excellency," or "His High Mightiness, the President of the United States and Protector of Their Liberties," a dispute that consumed John Adams and appalled

Madison—the debate over the chartering of the United States Bank divided Congress into bitter camps. As John Marshall wrote later in his life of Washington, "This measure made a deep impression on many members of the Legislature; and contributed not inconsiderably to the complete organization of those distinct and visible parties, which in their long and dubious conflict for power have since shaken the United States to their centre." The bank naturally appealed to those in favor of a strong government, who wished to interpret the Constitution constructively, so that it would be conducive to national greatness and commercial empire. The moneyed class, men of commercial intelligence, bondholders, merchants, speculators in securities—these men were in favor of the bank. The opponents of the bank were not necessarily dirt farmers, however; many of them, in fact, were businessmen and merchants who supported a decentralized banking system. They also included men who distrusted the powers of the national government, men who feared the creation of a class of dependents that would naturally seek to ingratiate itself with the government, and men who believed that the Federalists intended to establish a monarchy. Both those who had opposed and those who had endorsed the Constitution now attached themselves to it passionately and claimed to possess its authentic interpretation; the warring principles of the rival factions who contended over ratification were not reconciled but were displaced into the question of the document's meaning. It is a political dialectic that has continued to the present day.

Alexander Hamilton wished that the Constitution could

have simply abolished states and established a new national government in their stead—he wanted a fresh start, a clean slate, a "year zero." Consequently, he sought to interpret the document in such a way that the states would be denigrated and rendered inferior, since they so clearly conflicted with his thoroughly modern and modernizing view of what was required in order to make the new United States a prosperous economy and a great world power. Madison, joined by Thomas Jefferson, saw the Constitution as a means of checking the dangerous ambitions of Hamilton's absolutism. But it was not at all the case that these two men were opposed to banks and banking. They were suspicious of credit, and they did their best to separate the bank from direct government control, but in the end the management of the national economy and the pressures of international politics demanded that they adapt, and so they eventually did.

But those compromises and adaptations lay in the future. On April 9, 1792, William Branch Giles, a congressman from Virginia, rose in the House and delivered an address that crystallized the growing opposition to the Federalist agenda. He described Hamilton's program in dire terms, saying that it was a "powerful machine" designed to stimulate the inequality of wealth by placing the means to great fortunes in the hands of "a great moneyed interest" that would henceforth be "nurseries of immediate dependents upon the Government, whose interest will always stimulate them to support its measures, however iniquitous and tyrannical, and, indeed, the very emoluments which will compose the price of their attachment to the Government will grow out of a tyrannical violation of the rights of others." These dependents, please note, were not to be understood in the manner of modern American conservatives whose minds are filled with horror at the thought that destitute unmarried women might receive modest support from the state for their dependent children. These dependents were the stockjobbers, speculators, and financiers whose great fortunes would arise as a result of government debt and government spending, the spiritual ancestors of companies like the House of Morgan, Halliburton, General Electric, Exelon, and Goldman Sachs. Thus would the executive, having placed the control of these new moneyed resources as far as possible from the legislature, chart its own course, free from the deliberations of the people's representatives, secure with its new financial constituency. Giles concluded by observing that the new republic "was now in a state of puberty." The question was the nature of its future character. Would the republic "preserve the simplicity, chastity, and purity of her native representation and Republicanism, in which alone the true dignity and greatness of her character must consist?"—or, "so early in youth, prostitute herself to the venal and borrowed artifices and corruptions of a stale and pampered monarchy?"

Madison himself joined the struggle with a series of anonymous essays in the *National Gazette*, a republican sheet edited by the poet Philip Freneau, whom Madison and Jefferson had brought to the capital to counteract the influence of the Federalist *Gazette of the United States*. In one essay, "Parties," Madison presents, with magnificent concision, an encapsulation of his theory of interest and its relation to party:

In every political society, parties are unavoidable. A difference of interests, real or supposed is the most natural and fruitful source of them. The great objects should be to combat the evil: 1. By establishing political equality among all. 2. By withholding *unnecessary* opportunities from a few, to increase the inequality of property, by an immoderate, and especially unmerited, accumulation of riches. 3. By the silent operation of laws, which, without violating the rights of property, reduce extreme wealth towards a state of mediocrity, and raise extreme indigence towards a state of comfort. 4. By abstaining from measures which operate differently on different interests, and particularly such as favor one interest, at the expense of another. 5. By making one party a check on the other, so far as the existence of parties cannot be prevented, nor their views accommodated.—If this is not the language of reason, it is that of republicanism.

As he had argued in *The Federalist*, Madison maintains that natural parties or factions derive from different economic interests, which inevitably arise in society from the diverse and various modes of men's economic life. Since, as Madison wrote in 1787, "liberty is to faction, what air is to fire, an aliment, without which it instantly expires," the cure for the disease of party, extinguishing its ground in liberty, is far worse than the disease. The aim of government is to moderate its effects and to prevent the emergence of parties that are so powerful that they might come to overpower all others. If any such party were to obtain predominance over the state, it would naturally become a judge in its own cause and favor its own interests.

Out of such reflections and concerns had arisen the divided powers of the U.S. Constitution, a device that was not, as in much previous republican constitutional theory, an attempt to balance the natural monocratic, aristocratic, and democratic orders of society, but a scheme for dispersing the manifold and dynamic interests that necessarily arise within the abundance of competing economic interests of the people as a whole. Madison saw, in Hamilton's financial program, a plan to give preferential treatment to a particular mercantile and moneyed interest, in order to bind it tightly to the executive's energetic agenda. His rhetoric is withering, and his weapon of choice is devastating irony. He summarizes his opponents' views in the following manner: "In all political societies, different interests and parties arise out of the nature of things, and the great art of politicians lies in making them checks and balances to each other. Let us then increase these natural distinctions by favoring an inequality of property. . . . We shall then have the more checks to oppose to each other; we shall then have the more scales and the more weights to protect and maintain the equilibrium."

The language here is very close to his own, yet the distinctions make all the difference. He shows how a slight shift, using the vocabulary of American republicanism, in this case the doctrine of checks and balances, can be made to pervert republican ends. "From the expediency, in politics, of making natural parties, mutual checks on each other, to infer the propriety of creating artificial parties, in order to form them into mutual checks, is not less absurd than it would be in ethics, to say, that new vices ought to be promoted, where they would counteract each other, because this use may be made of existing vices." The Hamiltonian program, then, was objectionable because it identified and advanced a particular interest—that of the stockjobbers, brokers, speculators, and other capitalists—whose support in raising funds would be advantageous in advancing the powers of the central government. By doing so, the government would alter the balance of property and wealth in ways that were not only unnecessary but corrupting, particularly because this imbalance would naturally tend to draw men with such interests into government itself; they would not be content merely to feed at the public trough.

EXAMPLES OF THIS SORT OF corruption were readily available, as in the case of William Duer. Duer, an old associate of Hamilton, had been the secretary of the Board of Treasury of the Continental Congress prior to the formation of the new central government. He was the very model of the corrupt government official. Duer, born like Hamilton in the West Indies, was a speculator and sometime army contractor who always kept a host of deals in play; he often used his office to his advantage, even going so far as to mingle his own funds and those of Congress to the point where they were difficult to reconcile. He used his knowledge to gain entry into deals that came before the board, collected fees and bribes from individuals having business with the government, and in one instance came close to forming an international banking company that would have used the French government's holdings of United States debt as its initial capital, a grandiose scheme that eventually failed when it was overtaken by the French Revolution. Duer was also an officer of the notorious Scioto Company, which sold land it did not own to Frenchmen and enticed them to immigrate to the Ohio country. His reputation as a wheeler-dealer didn't hurt his political prospects, however, and Hamilton enlisted Duer to write some of the Federalist essays, though they were rejected as unsuitable and published under the name Philo-Publius.

When the new government was formed and George Washington arrived in New York to take up his executive duties, Duer's wife, Kitty, helped plan Washington's reception, and Duer himself was involved in finding and furnishing a house for the new president. When Hamilton was appointed secretary of the Treasury, he immediately selected Duer, whose wife happened to be a cousin of Mrs. Hamilton, as his assistant secretary. Employees of the new Treasury Department were forbidden to trade in public securities, but Duer quickly made it known to his business associates that he had no intention of abiding by that prohibition. During the debate over assumption of the states' debts he borrowed heavily, entered into various partnerships, and bought every state certificate he could lay hands on. Nor did he simply buy them and hope for appreciation or federal assumption of the debt, as many did; very much in the manner of modern currency or derivatives traders, Duer speculated on short-term fluctuations in price, created and exploited artificial shortages, and was constantly making deals and borrowing to pay the interest on older loans. In less than a year, Hamilton—who, fearing adverse publicity, had already intervened to prevent a lawsuit against his assistant—bowed to necessity and accepted Duer's resignation before his activities could permanently sink the chances of the funding program in Congress. Duer was forced out, but he had succeeded in elevating his status both nationally and internationally. He was the father of the revolving door, and into his footsteps more than 200 years later stepped men like Robert Rubin and Tom Daschle.

Duer soon became involved in Hamilton's Society for Establishing Useful Manufacturers, a new corporation that was the primary intended beneficiary of Hamilton's plan to promote domestic industry, soliciting stock subscriptions from his fellow New Yorkers and lobbying on the company's behalf to secure a corporate charter from the state of New Jersey. Duer and a group of New York speculators took control of the firm, and he was elected governor, the equivalent of chairman and CEO. He immediately began using the new company as a base for speculation, both in the corporation's own stock and in government securities. When, over Madison's objections and strenuous efforts, the charter of the Bank of the United States was successfully passed by Congress in February 1791, Duer naturally was in on the action. The first sale of the bank's stock on July 4 of that year in Boston, New York, and Philadelphia nearly caused a riot. Duer managed to buy up a large quantity of options to purchase the new stock, and before long those options had appreciated by 1,200 percent. When the bubble burst, as was inevitable, Hamilton intervened to support the market, and much of his spending directly benefited his old colleague. Hamilton's bailout enabled Duer to stay in business and set the stage for a broader crisis that affected the entire economy.

Duer's downfall came in a complex speculation that seems to have had its origins, at least in part, in a bet over whether Hamilton's new Bank of the United States would merge with the Bank of New York or buy it outright. Either way, a branch was coming to New York, and the rumors were generating speculative interest. Duer, who dropped the secretary's name at every opportunity, was thought to be in the know. Duer enlisted as a partner (though like many a modern speculator he put up none of his own money) a rich land speculator, Alexander Macomb, who was inexperienced in the stock markets, to buy Bank of New York stock on the assumption of a steep rise once Hamilton's decision was made public. What Macomb didn't know was that Duer was simultaneously selling his own shares, taking advantage of the market that Macomb was making with his purchases, and setting a standard of lowdown behavior that has continued to the present, as the SEC's lawsuit against Goldman Sachs attests. The dealings went ever deeper, and more partners were brought in, on both sides of the market, as Duer was forced to cover his notes with new loans, many of which were taken out at usurious rates. A new bubble was created, and according to some accounts Duer attempted to corner the market on 6 percent government bonds. Finally, in March 1792, the Bank of New York stopped lending, possibly because a rival financial combination was shorting the market and withdrawing specie from the bank to create a credit shortage. The strategy seems to have worked: credit contracted severely, and the bubble burst.

The Panic of 1792 was the first Wall Street crash, and it created a severe depression. Not only were credit markets disrupted but money itself was hard to come by. Work ceased on building projects, prices fell, and men lost their jobs. Duer was thrown into debtors' prison. Mobs attempted to storm the jail, throwing stones at the building and chanting, "We will have Mr. Duer, he has gotten our money." Many of Duer's partners and cosigners fled New York; others ended up in prison; some came to blows with each other. The speculation had drawn in many merchants and other nonspeculators who treated stocks as an investment; there was so little money in circulation that farmers could not be paid for their wheat. One New Yorker wrote that "as for confidence there is no such thing, not a grocer can get credit for a hogshead of sugar or a puncheon of rum." Another complained that "in point of public & private distress nothing can exceed the present—a plague, famine, or fire perhaps could not have done so much evil." Thomas Jefferson wrote on March 16 that "Duer, the king of the alley, is under a sort of check. The stocksellers say he will rise again. The stock-buyers count him out, and the credit & fate of the nation seem to hang on the desperate throws & plunges of gambling scoundrels." To the same correspondent, in April, he reported the loss in New York to be $5 million, "which is reckoned the value of all the buildings of the city: so that if the whole town had been burnt to the ground it would have been just the measure of the present calamity." Boston, he said, had suffered a loss of $1 million. "In the mean time, buildings & other improvements are suspended. Workmen turned adrift. Country produce not to be sold at any price: because even substantial merchants, who never medelled with paper, cannot tell how many of their debtors have medelled & may fail: consequently they are afraid to make any new money arrangements till they shall know how they stand. As much of the demand from Virginia, & especially for wheat, & indeed tobacco, is from this place, I imagine the stagnation of purchases, & trouble of prices will reach you immediately."

Hamilton intervened aggressively to support the market, buying up government debt that was trading well below par; by the end of the year, the sinking fund had spent more than $364,000, half of which was used to manage the market rather than retire debt, the declared purpose of the fund. For Madison and Jefferson, this episode was merely proof of what they had foretold. Duer's bubble came close to destroying Hamilton's new system of finance. Duer—so reminiscent in his personal character of Bernard Madoff and other famous Wall Street villains down through history, and in his intimacy with government a foreshadowing of a long line of Goldman Sachs grandees—never recovered. Reforms followed, including the founding of a public stock exchange, the forerunner of the New York Stock Exchange. But as Obama learned when sitting at the knee of Robert Rubin, capitalism does not stand still for long. Like the poor, the William Duers of the world will always be with us.

★ ★ ★

THE OPPOSITION PARTY THAT JEFFERSON and Madison formed was animated by a well-articulated political philosophy, yet it quickly attracted adherents who were less concerned with the fine points of republican principles than with their own economic interests. This was not a contradiction or an inconsistency—indeed, it was perfectly in keeping with Madison's theory of interest. The Republican Party's supporters were not only the traditional agrarian interests of the Southern planters and freehold farmers of all sections but rising commercial and social interests throughout the states who were constrained and excluded by the established mercantile interests of the Federalists and their allies. Some of the new Republicans were religious or ethnic minorities: Baptists in New England who disliked the Congregationalists, Germans, the Scots-Irish, and others who resented the Anglophile "powderhead" aristocrats, old Tories, and socialites who made up the Federalist elite. Northern and mid-Atlantic Republicans included salaried employees and laborers as well as merchants who traded not with the British, as did the Federalists, but with the French, the West Indies, China, India, Germany, and other parts of Continental Europe. Many wealthy manufacturers and "middling" artisans discovered that Hamilton's program for domestic industry was halfhearted at best, since he was far more interested in finance than in fostering a manufacturing sector, and the duties placed on imports did not go far enough to protect their businesses from British competition. When the Federalists imposed excise taxes on domestic products, many artisans, tradesmen, and manufacturers took to the streets in protest and soon lined up behind the Republican opposition. Thus the Republicans had on their side the energetic rising entrepreneurial classes, many of whose members were already quite wealthy but were considered by the Federalist elite to be an ignorant lower-class rabble. Alexander Hamilton, and the Federalists as a party, had wagered their political survival on a narrow oligarchy of Anglophile merchants and paper men. Ultimately, they made a bad bet.

The Quasi-War with France in 1798–1800, coming as it did in the midst of the French revolutionary wars, created a panic not unlike the one that seized the United States in the aftermath of the attacks of September 11, 2001. Anti-French and anti-immigrant hysteria gripped the nation, and the Federalists believed or pretended to believe that the ranks of the Republicans, who had long expressed their sympathies with France over England, were filled with spies and Jacobins. Congress, now with a Federalist majority, and with Madison having retired to Virginia, passed a series of laws that have come to be known as the Alien and Sedition Acts of 1798, which established a series of precedents that despite challenges to their constitutionality have been replayed in one way or another throughout our history. The acts gave the president the sole and arbitrary authority to judge that an alien was a threat to the United States and to expel him without trial. Adams justified the law by claiming that "French Spies then swarmed in our Cities and in the Country." The government prepared lists of foreigners for deportation; when one, a refugee from the Reign of Terror who had opened a bookstore in Philadelphia, conveyed a personal appeal to the president asking why he was being targeted, Adams was said to have replied: "Nothing in particular, but he's too French."

Thousands of French immigrants fled the country. It was not an accident that bookstore owners and editors were targeted; like the Bushite Republicans after 9/11, the Federalists were using hysteria—in this case, anti-French hysteria—in an attempt to damage their partisan opponents. Jefferson's Republicans responded with outrage, though there was little at the time that they could do, since judicial review had yet to be established and the courts were in the hands of Federalists anyway. Jefferson observed that the Alien Friends Act was "a most detestable thing," something that belonged more properly to the eighth or ninth century. The Sedition Act, especially, made it obvious that the Republicans and not a hypothetical mass of French spies were the true target of the suppression; under this act, it was illegal to "write, print, utter or publish," or cause or procure or aid such "writing, uttering or publishing" of anything "false, scandalous and malicious" against the government, or the Congress, with either intent to harm or intent to bring them into "contempt or disrepute." Notably excluded from protection under the law was the vice presidency, the office held by Thomas Jefferson, and the act was made to expire at the end of Adams's term. Benjamin Franklin Bache, the editor of the *Aurora*, a vigorously pro-Republican paper, was among the first targets of prosecution and indeed was arrested even before Adams signed the bill into law. After Bache died of yellow fever, William Duane, his successor both as editor and as husband, was also targeted. Most of the others who were convicted were also Republican journalists.

Even Hamilton was disturbed by the persecuting fever of the Federalists. "Let us not establish a tyranny," he wrote to Oliver Wolcott, upon seeing an early draft of the Sedition Act. "Energy is a very different thing from violence. If we make no false step, we shall be essentially united, but if we push things to an extreme, we shall then give to faction *body* and solidity." He was correct in this assessment, and the backlash from the persecution helped propel Jefferson into the presidency and ultimately contributed to the collapse of the Federalist Party.

Some historians have argued that the Republicans, by appropriating the Whiggish ideology of English opposition thought, had developed a conspiratorial ideology full of "hysterical fears and fantastic predictions," and saw nonexistent plots to overthrow liberty and establish a monocratic regime. The Federalist persecution, the "reign of the witches" as Jefferson put it, demonstrates otherwise. Much is made by others of the great historical irony that the Republicans, once they came into power in 1800, did little to retard the growth of state banks. In 1791, when Hamilton created the Bank of the United States, the Federalists were a small plutocracy in control of the government. There were only three banks in the United States. By 1811, when the Republicans killed the Bank of the United States, the Federalists had been out of power for eleven years and their party was in collapse, and there were ninety banks in the United States. By 1820 there were more than 300. And in 1816, as no one ever fails to point out, President Madison was obliged to acquiesce in the rechartering of the U.S. Bank to finance the debt resulting from the War of 1812. Madison came to see that Hamilton was correct about the need for more vigorous management of the economy, but he never compromised his opposition to Hamilton's paper men or adopted his rival's view of executive power.

Undeniably, Hamilton had been trying to corrupt the government by cultivating a moneyed class dependent on it. Hamilton quite self-consciously saw himself as a kind of prime minister and based his administration on that of Robert Walpole in England, the classic example of ministerial corruption for Country party polemics. His thinking can be seen as an American version of the eighteenth-century Court tradition, perhaps best captured in David Hume's historical and political writings, which held that classical republican virtue was too demanding and unrealistic. Rather than insist on the austere requirements of republican participation in the public life of the state, Daniel Defoe, Hume, Adam Smith, and other thinkers who followed in this tradition argued that commerce was a better vehicle for the development of citizens' civic personalities and that a certain amount of corruption in government, and thus in society, was unavoidable. They argued that the growth of commerce would exercise a softening and civilizing influence on society as citizens pursued their private interests; rather than the ideal of civic virtue, an emphatically public and republican ideal, these thinkers valued politeness and manners, virtues of private life and personal cultivation. The fate of the arts and letters (if not the sciences) in the capitalistic order that ensued, which canonized Adam Smith as its preeminent prophet, is decidedly ironic, as is the resemblance of this optimistic commercial ideal to Marx's utopian vision of the society of free and associated producers.

Hamilton left a large body of writings that attests to his ambitions for the new American state, and though he described himself as a republican, he made no secret of his anti-democratic views, which were not exactly unusual at the time; like his ally John Adams, he subscribed to a far more English and aristocratic version of a mixed constitution. Madison was also a close reader of Hume and Smith, and his thinking was powerfully influenced by their critique of classical republican virtue, but he drew different conclusions regarding the excellence of the British system, and he would not have forgotten Hamilton's speeches before the convention in 1787, in one of which he described the English constitution as the finest in all the world. "All communities," Hamilton declared, "divide themselves into the few and the many. The first are the rich and well-born, the other the mass of the people. The voice of the people has been said to be the voice of God; and, however generally this maxim has been quoted and believed, it is not true in fact. The people are turbulent and changing; they seldom judge or determine right. Give, therefore, to the first class a distinct, permanent share in the government. They will check the unsteadiness of the second, and, as they cannot receive any advantage by a change, they therefore will ever maintain good government." Hamilton was indeed in favor of something very like an elective monarchy. "And let me observe," he continued in the same speech, "that an Executive is less dangerous to the liberties of the people when in office during life, than for seven years. It may be said, this constitutes an elective monarchy. Pray, what is a monarchy? May not the governors of the respective States be considered in that light? But, by making the Executive subject to impeachment, the term monarchy cannot apply."

To republicans like Jefferson and Madison, Hamilton's contempt for democratic principles was heretical to the spirit of the new union—even if Madison was far from being an advocate of simple or direct democracy, which he always believed was liable to end as a tyranny of the majority. The overriding concern of Madison's constitutional philosophy was the construction of a republic that would persist as such through history and thus avoid the fate, considered inevitable by most thinkers from Aristotle to Montesquieu, of degenerating into a corrupt and intolerable despotism. Although Hamilton was by all accounts remarkably free of any personal mercenary ambitions, at least by eighteenth-century standards, it cannot be denied that he believed some degree of corruption was necessary in order to bind the "*immediate* interests of the moneyed men to cooperate with government" as he put it in a letter to the financier Robert Morris in 1780, when he was still serving as Washington's aide during the war. As his writings—and his association with men such as Duer—make clear, he fully intended to bind moneyed men to the state through patronage, mutual influence, and shared interest.

Even if we grant that Hamilton personally was a kind of incorruptible saint, and that his antagonism was directed primarily against anything smacking of localism and disunity, it may yet be the case that he was mistaken in the end about the interests and power of his "moneyed men." Madison, for his part, was able to see that what Hamilton sought to attract and control was one moneyed interest among many. This dependency or mutual entanglement of the government and a strong, selfish private interest was precisely what Madison feared, because it would lead to one of two very undesirable outcomes: either an overpowering executive would be able to assimilate the entire body of government to itself and thus subvert constitutional balance; or, by giving the paper interest of stockjobbers and speculators an effective veto power over the government's large policies—in contemporary terms, its macroeconomic, fiscal, and monetary policies—the state would come to serve the narrow interest of that faction. One path led to a kind of monarchy, whether or not the executive be called a king; the other to an oligarchy.

Moreover, despite their polemics and principled disapproval of speculators and other paper men, and despite Jefferson's most quotable sentences, it is not at all the case that Jefferson and Madison were opposed to commerce. Even if Jefferson was personally repelled by financial abstraction in most of its forms, his embrace or at least tolerance of state banks was not necessarily an inconsistency. Credit itself might be a necessity, but *public* credit, in their view, was an engine of government that should be avoided if at all possible. They were not proto-socialists, though they did, in keeping with a powerful strain of republican thought, insist that a balance of property must be maintained, that one element of society should not become so wealthy that it could assimilate the state to itself or withdraw behind iron gates and neglect the community at large. It is as unnatural and contrary to liberty for the state to depend on the grace and patronage of the wealthy as for the wealthy to depend on the patronage of the state.

Nor was poverty the ideal, because poverty and indigence also tended to create dependency, and no one who was dependent on the will of another could be said to be free. The goal was to create laws that operated silently to discourage great disparities in property and wealth, without violating the rights of property, on which, after all, republican society was based.

In no way was this a utopian political philosophy. Madison's vision of the state was primarily that of a disinterested umpire of competing interests, but for such a state to survive required a vigilant maintenance of the republican point of view, with each branch of government jealously guarding its powers against the inevitable encroachment of the others, and the public itself watchful over the whole. He distrusted any interest that might grow so powerful as to overawe all others, and for this reason saw "incorporated societies"—corporations—as a particular threat. Hamilton, in contrast, regarded the state itself as the preeminent and supreme interest, and he trusted the self-interest of the moneyed few to keep it from degenerating into despotism. He wished to be the founder of a great empire; his motivation above all was the prospect of everlasting glory, both personal and national. Even after the Panic of 1792, Madison and Jefferson were unable to prevent the enactment of Hamilton's program; the secretary of the Treasury had the votes in Congress as well as Washington's ear and his broad sympathy when it came to executive power. And although Madison and Jefferson narrowly succeeded in gaining control of the government in an election that was thrown to the House of Representatives, they found that history was not on their side. Despite his personal misfortunes—disgraced, driven from office, murdered in a duel—it was Hamilton who won in the end.

Today, with obvious and enormous differences, we still live inside the dialectic established during those original debates concerning the nature of the federal Constitution and the proper scope of executive power. Our constitutional disagreements keep circling back to those that were dramatized between the two most outstanding intellects of the revolutionary generation—and not only in the domain of public finance. Challenges to ObamaCare are likely to be made on the basis of the Tenth Amendment, and the still unresolved arguments concerning the dangerous Reagan-Bush doctrine of the unitary executive, state secrets, war powers, and detention policy all have distinct echos of the arguments that raged in the 1790s. Even if we resist the austere Machiavellian imperative that a republic must periodically return to first principles, it often happens that we recapitulate those principles in one way or another whether we wish to or not.

CHAPTER SIX

THE GREATEST
WEALTH IS HEALTH

The passage of the health-care bill in March 2010 no doubt saved Obama's flailing presidency, at least in the eyes of the media; it also suggested the likely outcome of the finance reform legislation. Barring some act of God, whatever ends up passing will be weak, with the most valuable proposals either completely sacrificed in negotiations—just like the public option, prescription-drug importation, and the Medicare buy-in provision—or watered down and laden with so many compromises, exceptions, loopholes, and carve-outs that it will do little to address the fundamental absurdities of the current system.

During the dark days of winter, in the immediate after-math of Senator Scott Brown's victory in Massachusetts, last rites were being muttered in Washington for health-care legislation that had already passed both the House and the Senate, with Democrats like Barney Frank and Anthony Weiner declaring that the Senate bill had no hope of being passed in the House. Long-established parliamentary tactics such as budget reconciliation and deem-and-pass, which were used repeatedly by the Republicans in those rare instances when the Democrats tried to deny Bush some legislative tidbit, were preemptively ruled out for being inordinately polarizing or partisan or at least cumbersome and difficult. The White House began to show signs of factionalism and palace intrigue, and various actors from within the administration began to seed the political press with propaganda designed to salvage reputations and cast blame on rivals. Most notably, there was an eruption of pieces centering on Rahm Emanuel, Obama's thuggish chief of staff. (A similar rash of profiles celebrated the heroic and unprecedented accomplishments of Timothy Geithner.) Some of the articles blamed the entire Chicago cohort of advisers, including Emanuel, David Axelrod, Robert Gibbs, and Valerie Jarrett, for the debacle. This critique demanded the firing of Emanuel, claiming that he was incapable of running the White House and that he was preventing Obama from being Obama. What else could explain the fundamental messaging failures, the inability to fashion a coherent and compelling *narrative* to explain to the American people why this health-care bill was so essential to Obama's agenda of change and hope?

Other stories, no doubt planted by Emanuel himself or

by close allies, and in noticeably more prominent venues such as the *Washington Post*, cast the chief of staff as a hard-core realist who was unable to rein in Obama's idealism. According to that story line, Emanuel had advocated a minimalist approach to health reform, with a focus on uncontroversial measures that Republicans would have difficulty opposing. Seeking absolution for Emanuel from other allegedly blame-worthy PR debacles, this argument contended that he had also opposed a civilian trial for Khalid Sheikh Mohammed and had battled against the White House counsel Gregory Craig over the president's campaign promise to close Guan-tánamo (a battle Craig supposedly won, though the prison camp remains open and Craig was forced out in November 2009). Moreover, Axelrod, Jarrett, and Gibbs were said to be Obama cultists too much in love with the great man to offer him good advice.

Variations on the theme soon surfaced everywhere in the press. Obituaries for the administration were sprouting up on every political blog, and the comparisons swiftly reached beyond the Clinton administration to that of the lamentable Jimmy Carter. Most of the criticism was directed at Obama's advisers, but there were worrying signs that the crisis was beginning to damage the main brand itself—that the press, which hates nothing so much as perceived weakness in the White House, was on the verge of decisively repudiating its darling. Personal critiques emerged, even if they centered on failures of messaging and narrative framing. All agreed, Obama's halo was fading.

Most of the media activity was a by-product of the battle within the Democratic party over how to proceed after the debacle in Massachusetts; it continued until a deal was struck. Finally, in March, Speaker of the House Nancy Pelosi rescued the Democrats from their natural instincts—the temptation to scale back their ambitions and try to find some minimal compromise with the Republicans—and forced Obama to put his presidency on the line for the bill. The resulting Democratic victory may or may not have improved the party's discouraging midterm prospects, but it certainly transformed the worrying media narrative into one of triumph and legislative brilliance on a par with that of LBJ and FDR. But to trumpet the corrupt result as a great liberal triumph, a historic refashioning of the American health-care system, is merely to repeat the Democrats' wishful narrative. The health bill is of a piece with Obama's general approach to governance, which is to make loud, dramatic claims about his purportedly reformist agenda—claims that both his supporters and his enemies almost always take at face value—while working behind the scenes to ensure that no major stakeholder in his coalition of corporate backers will suffer significant losses.

The health bill that was signed on March 23 is best understood as a bailout of the private health industry that seeks to guarantee some 30 million additional customers for insurance companies and continued obscene profits for large drug manufacturers. Almost everyone in the health-industrial complex will get paid in one way or another. Far from reshaping our patently insane system, ObamaCare merely entrenches its most irrational elements, and though the law contains praiseworthy measures that mitigate some of the most harmful insurance practices, in broad terms it merely postpones the kind of fundamental reforms that our broken health-care system demands.

THE MOOD WAS JUBILANT IN the East Room of the White House when President Obama and Vice President Biden strode in with their big smiles, the spectators chanting, "Fired up! Ready to go! Fired up! Ready to go!" Biden immediately felt a need to call attention to the fact that politicians always claim their legislative accomplishments are "historic," that the American people had won a great victory, and that the forces of darkness—at last!—were overcome when we passed *this extremely important bill.* Historic, he said. And history isn't just what's printed in books—history is what people do: "History is made when men and women decide that there is a greater risk in accepting a situation that we cannot bear than in steeling our spine and embracing the promise of change. That's when history is made." History is made when a great and fearless leader matches passion with principle and charts a new course, and that leader, he said, smiling at Obama, who was standing by his side, is you. You are the one. All those great men of the past, beginning with Teddy Roosevelt and ending with Teddy Kennedy, tried and fell short. "You have turned, Mr. President, the right of every American to have access to decent health care into reality for the first time in American history."

Obama was pleased and his bearing was proud. He had reason to be pleased, of course, because his presidency had just been saved from what would probably have been a fatal defeat. But the idea that his bill enshrines a right to decent health care is, quite simply, false. The vice president was lying, though he may not have realized it, since by the time a politician rises to Joe Biden's mendacious stature, he has long ago lost the ability to distinguish fact from even the cheapest propaganda. A statutory requirement that all adult citizens must purchase an insurance policy from a predatory for-profit business that adds no value to the economic transaction accompanying the activities of doctors and nurses simply does not measure up to the Declaration of the Rights of Man or the first ten amendments to the Constitution of the United States. And not by any means does requiring people to purchase an insurance policy guarantee decent health care. It is what it is: a government mandate, a legal requirement, an obligation to purchase what is essentially a financial product. A tax, in other words and by other means—a tax that in essence guarantees a profit for a private corporation, which now enjoys a state-sanctioned monopoly.

Nor is such mandatory insurance, as Biden asserted, a "final girder" in the "framework for a social network," whatever that might mean, to give people the "most important element" of what they need: "access to good health." Such clumsy rhetoric testifies to the debased state of our national discourse. Too many American public figures, and not just appalling cyborgs like Joe Biden, natter on about "access" to "good health," as if health were a commodity to be purchased at some horrifying strip mall in a retail shop run by Wellpoint or United HealthCare. Health is not a product, and it's certainly not a product of insurance. Health, setting aside such contingencies as genetics and accidents, arises from one's way of being in the world, from habits of diet and physical activity that transcend competitive markets and allegedly well-meaning legislation. And this whole spectrum of American life—including especially our society's refusal to accept that inactivity and government-subsidized foodlike substances lead to epidemic rates of obesity and diabetes—is mostly ignored by this woolly mammoth of a bill.

In a final curlicue, Biden felt the need to quote a poet, since the occasion was so auspicious and he loves to quote poets in all kinds of interesting contexts. "Look, the classic poet, Virgil, once said that 'The greatest wealth is health.' The greatest wealth is health. Well, today, America becomes a whole lot wealthier because tens of millions of Americans will be a whole lot healthier from this moment on." Although Virgil may well have said something along those lines, he never wrote it—at least not according to scholars contacted by Meghan Clyne of the *Weekly Standard*, who also helpfully reminds us of this classic mingle-mangle of Bidenisms, uttered during the Sage of Wilmington's run for the presidency in 1988:

> I think I probably have a much higher IQ than you do, I suspect. I went to law school on a full academic scholarship—the only one in my class to have a full academic scholarship. . . . I won the international moot court competition. I was the outstanding student in the political science department at the end of my year.

I graduated with three degrees from undergraduate school, and 165 credits—only needed 123—and I'd be delighted to sit down and compare my IQ to yours.

Poor Biden—much like Sarah Palin, he just can't help himself, though for some reason his gaffes, blunders, and outright lies never seem to attract the dedicated attention that has been lavished on George W. Bush and Dick Cheney.

Obama, on the other hand, was somewhat more subdued and tasteful in his remarks. He immediately reached for the upper registers of his political rhetoric, but unlike his hapless vice president, Obama—in voice and bearing—was up to the task: "Today, after almost a century of trying; today, after over a year of debate; today, after all the votes have been tallied—health insurance reform becomes law in the United States of America. [Applause.] Today." Those things are all more or less true in a narrow sense. We have been trying for more than 100 years to enact a system of national health care in this country; and we have suffered through a year of debate; but today, after the votes are tallied and the bill becomes law and the lobbyists get to work shaping the implementation of the new regulations—today, we are not yet a modern civilized country with national health care. Today. Obama and the Democrats did succeed in passing "health insurance reform," of that there can be no doubt. But this reform of insurance, which will to its credit seek to prohibit some of the most egregious and inhumane practices of these parasitic corporations, does not constitute fundamental reform of our health-care system.

The spectators were a friendly crowd, so it wasn't hard to get them worked up. They had just won a famous victory, after all, but there was something farcical about the marriage of high rhetoric with insurance jargon such as tax credits, incentives, preexisting conditions, lifetime maximums, and Medicare doughnut holes. Thank God that children with asthma and brain cancer will be able to get insurance, but their parents won't necessarily be able to afford what it costs if, like 8 million of their fellow Americans, they happen to have lost their jobs. The bill does nothing to reduce the absolute dependency on employers for health-care security that our system imposes on most American citizens. And given Obama's shameful retreat from his repeated campaign promises to include a public plan to compete with the predations of the insurance companies, his grandiose closing cadences were so offensive as to be obscene: "We are a nation that faces its challenges and accepts its responsibilities. We are a nation that does what is hard. What is necessary. What is right. Here, in this country, we shape our own destiny. That is what we do. That is who we are. That is what makes us the United States of America." It was curious to notice a slight little soft-shoe shift in Obama's closing, a minor fudge that revealed a dim (or devious, depending on your point of view) awareness that what he was claiming in his little speech was not matching up very well with the mundane reality of the deals that were made early on with the health-care industry: "And we have now just enshrined, as soon as I sign this bill, the core principle that everybody should have some basic security when it comes to their health care." Note the fudge: not "basic security" but "*some* basic security." It's a small thing, that "some," but through it one can drive large semitrucks laden with corporate subsidies and giveaways.

The liberal press dutifully played its role in the political drama, helpfully repeating to its loyal readers that the bill was historic, a great triumph, the most significant social legislation to pass Congress in a generation. It was indeed a famous victory. In a front-page encomium, David Leonhardt of the *New York Times* declared that "the bill that President Obama signed on Tuesday is the federal government's biggest attack on economic inequality since inequality began rising more than three decades ago." This explains, he said, why the president dared to spend his political capital so recklessly on an issue that did "not appear to be his top priority as a presidential candidate." Most Americans, on the contrary, probably did think that health-care reform was a central priority for Obama during his candidacy, but what ties everything together for Leonhardt is the idea that Obama is making a "deliberate effort" to bring the "age of Reagan" to a close—an effort that cannot fail to come as a surprise to anyone who has closely followed Obama's utterances on the subject of the fortieth president of the United States. Leonhardt tells us that nothing so sweeping has been enacted on Capitol Hill since the passage of Medicare in 1965 and that long drift of inequality in America over the last three decades, a period in which "real incomes at the 99.99th percentile have jumped more than 300 percent since 1980," is now coming to an end, thanks to Obama's health reform. During this same period, he tells us, the median household income rose less than 15 percent.

This long desperate trend of ever-growing inequality, for which he magnanimously absolves, without explanation, Reagan's "laissez-faire revolution," is now coming to an end because "a big chunk" of the cost for the plan comes from taxes on the wealthy, while many benefits will allegedly flow toward people closer to the poverty level. Taxpayers with incomes over $1 million will pay an average of $46,000 more in taxes, he says, though it's hard to believe that people earning $1 million a year will feel much of a pinch, or that they will really end up paying those taxes, since everyone knows that taxable income, for the rich, is notoriously "elastic," especially considering the fact that Reagan did not entirely stamp out the market for tax shelters that bothered Obama so much in *The Audacity of Hope*. It's hard to see how a very modest tax increase on the richest tippy-top percentage of Americans will do a whole lot to bring the age of Reagan to an end.

The upside for poor and middle-income Americans, however, is much harder to pinpoint. As a handful of critics have assiduously pointed out, ObamaCare is largely based on the Massachusetts state plan proposed by Mitt Romney, which, as Nancy Pelosi herself acknowledged in a memo she distributed on March 21, drew heavily on ideas from the right-wing Heritage Foundation. As part of her fact sheet, Pelosi included a *Washington Post* column by E. J. Dionne that stated with admirable directness that the Democrats' plan was, in essence, a Republican plan. ObamaCare relies on so-called market principles. In the perverse language of Washington, this means not that it creates an undistorted, non-monopolistic, competitive marketplace but rather that it preserves the ability of private monopolies to skim large profits from the system: it preserves the parasitism of insurance companies, and it compels middle-class people without employer-sponsored health care to pay at least as much for insurance as they pay in federal income taxes. Pelosi's staff apparently believed that publicizing the Republican character of the Democratic plan was good politics—it showed how intransigent and obstructive her opponents were being in refusing to vote for a model they themselves invented. Perhaps it was good politics, but it also unintentionally revealed how bankrupt and spineless were the Democrats for failing to include anything that might reasonably be called progressive in their triumphant, historic, game-changingly awesome legislation that adds the last girder to Joe Biden's social network.

Indeed, the drug and insurance industries supported this bill from the very beginning, as did the hospital associations, the American Medical Association, medical equipment manufacturers, and practically anyone else who has a stake in profit-driven health care. Most notoriously, Obama and the Democrats made a secret deal with the pharmaceutical industry, agreeing to limit the reduction in its profits to $80 billion, or about 3 percent of its current drug profits over ten years, in return for its support. The drug lobby, PhRMA, pledged to put $150 million worth of television advertisements behind the legislation. This backroom deal took place despite the fact that Obama, as a candidate, had actually run an ad, titled "Billy," attacking PhRMA's lead lobbyist, Billy Tauzin (the turncoat Blue Dog Democrat and former Republican chairman of the House Energy and Commerce Committee) for making a similar deal during the negotiations for Medicare

Part D. America's Health Insurance Plans (AHIP) also supported ObamaCare early on—I lost track of how many times I heard Karen Ignagni, this trade group's president, promoting the plan on talk shows—and spent millions supporting it, though AHIP and other erstwhile allies of the administration did oppose the legislation during the final stretch, in petulant outrage at not securing a strong enough insurance mandate. Unhappy with the final legislation, PhRMA fired Billy Tauzin from his job, which had paid $2 million a year.

There can be little doubt, however, that PhRMA and AHIP will work hand in glove with the administration and Congress to make sure the implementation of the plan is more to the industry's liking—and, of course, immediately after the bill was signed into law, AHIP and PhRMA both agreed to participate in a nationwide campaign, called Enroll America, to promote the new legislation. It's their law, after all. Senator Max Baucus's chief health aide was a former executive at Wellpoint (yes, the very company that achieved satanic renown for raising rates 39 percent at the height of the health-care drama) and Baucus's draft bill was reportedly leaked to lobbyists who used to be on his staff, before even the White House saw a copy. According to a report published in February 2010 by the Sunlight Foundation, "over the course of 2009, the drug-industry trade group spent over $28 million on in-house and hired lobbyists. Aside from PhRMA's massive in-house lobbying operation, the trade group hired 48 outside lobbying firms. The total number of lobbyists working for PhRMA in 2009 reached 165. Some 137 of those 165 lobbyists representing PhRMA were former employees of either the legislative or executive branches. Of these, dozens were former congressional staffers including two former chiefs of staff to Max Baucus." (Jim Messina, Obama's deputy chief of staff, was also formerly Baucus's chief of staff.) Those numbers were simply one small part of the overall lobbying picture with regard to health insurance reform. The pharmaceutical and health-products industry spent almost $268 million lobbying Congress in 2009, with 446 reported clients and 1,735 registered lobbyists; insurance companies spent more than $164 million; hospitals and nursing homes spent just under $108 million; health professionals spent $84 million; health services and HMOs spent almost $74 million. The health industry as a whole spent $545 million lobbying Congress in 2009.

IN THE *WALL STREET JOURNAL,* as one might expect, the reactions to the bill were somewhat different from those in the *Times.* But in addition to the usual Republican boilerplate, largely by-the-numbers political theater, and propaganda that one often finds in the *Journal*'s editorial pages, there were also some very smart deconstructions of the new system's most glaring flaws. Holman W. Jenkins Jr., for example, argued that ObamaCare "has ended up doubling down on the system's existing perversities." Jenkins patiently reminds his readers that the insurance industry was not Obama's enemy during the long health-care debate; just as with his halfhearted denunciation of "fat-cat bankers," Obama's tentative demonization of insurers was pure theater, mere role-playing that exploited the general public's ignorance of the hard cold facts. "But from the beginning," Jenkins writes, "the industry was his ally because he set out to solve its biggest problem—which is not the same as America's biggest problem." Wellpoint and the other health insurers, despite their unhappiness with the weak public mandate that all citizens become their customers, are still going to make money, money guaranteed by government subsidies. America will continue to pay too much for inferior care, and insurance companies no longer have to worry about their failing business model. The Internal Revenue Service hereafter will serve as the insurance industry's enforcer. Costs will go up as Medicare cuts are rescinded; the mandate will be strengthened; "more and more tax money will have to be found to keep the jalopy on the road."

By delaying implementation of the new law, the Democrats have cleverly engineered a steady flow of contributions from the health industry as it seeks to influence the final shape of new regulations. Despite all the numbers thrown around by smarty-pants on both sides of the fictional aisle, no one will really know what this bill will cost individuals and companies until the regulations are all written. The immediate announcements by large newsworthy firms such as Verizon that their health costs would be likely to increase by millions over the next few years, and the sizable write-downs by companies such as AT&T, Deere, and Caterpillar, were all attempts to leverage public opinion and influence the still shaky psyches of Democrats who couldn't quite believe they had the wherewithal to win such a big fight against Republicans. Yet it had to be admitted, even by Henry Waxman, that the health liabilities of large corporations would go up. (Just the elimination of one tax deduction for a federal subsidy on retirees' drug benefits was projected to cost the S&P 500 $4.5 billion in first-quarter earnings.) No matter what happens, however, health insurance, with all its perverse incentives, is still hardwired into the system, and insurance is still tied to employment, with the result that most Americans will remain dependent on the arbitrary power of employers for access to health care.

Jenkins rightly pointed out that the current system is failing. Why is it failing? Not merely because of the historical accident, brought about by postwar tinkering with the tax code, that gave American companies an incentive to offer health insurance to their employees, thus resulting in a tax loophole of $250 billion a year. The decision to exempt such compensation from payroll taxation was fatal to our system, because corporations have been unwilling, until recently, to consider giving up the federal government's subsidy of their labor costs, and the insurance industry was unwilling to see its cash cow led to slaughter. The more fundamental issue, however, is that health is simply not insurable.

Insurance is essentially a bet entered into between two parties that the insurable event will or will not happen. Homeowners' policies, for example, insure primarily against unlikely catastrophic events such as fires or floods. If you live in an area that is certain to be flooded, you will not be able to obtain private flood insurance at any cost, because it makes no sense for an insurance company to bet that you will not suffer a flood. If you're lucky, you'll get government flood insurance. Automobile insurance is similar: despite the fact that many people insure their cars for minor damage as well, the only form of car insurance that makes good economic sense is for catastrophic damage and liability. Insurance companies employ actuaries to make elaborate statistical forecasts of who is likely to suffer particular adverse events, and thus generate rates based on an individual's risk profile. Health insurance companies make their money by keeping sick people out of their pools, rationing care, and denying claims. They are not in the health-care business; they are in the claim-denying business. It makes as much economic sense to insure a sick person (that is, someone with a "preexisting condition") as it does to insure a house that is already on fire. Thus the unavoidable contradiction of "health insurance."

Shortly after I got out of college I worked as an insurance adjuster for a company in Florida that specialized in minimum car insurance policies for risky drivers. It was a non-standard auto insurance company; in this case, that simply meant it had significantly lower underwriting standards than a mainstream company such as GEICO. This company, which I'll call Fatal Insurance, had contrived a particularly devious business model. The state of Florida, like most states, required proof of insurance before you could drive off with a new car. This was a mandate, very much like our new health insurance mandate, although no one was forcing you to buy a car. Florida also had something very similar to an insurance exchange; it was known as an independent insurance broker, who had a license to sell insurance policies from different companies. If you went to an insurance broker in Miami, you would first be offered the standard policies from Allstate, GEICO, or Progressive; these were more expensive products and therefore carried a higher commission for the broker. But if you were poor and couldn't afford one of those so-called Cadillac plans, you asked for something cheaper. If you asked for the cheapest policy available or were a high-risk driver, you were likely to get something by Fatal Insurance. The insurance application included a number of questions, such as whether you'd been involved in any recent accidents, or whether you'd been cited for any moving violations, or whether your driver's license was suspended. If you had enough moving violations or accidents or your license was suspended, you weren't insurable at all, and thus you wouldn't be able to get title to that sweet little Chevy Caprice that was sitting on the lot down the road in Homestead.

If you lied on an application for a normal insurance company, the broker would find out right away, because a standard company required its salespeople to run the customer's DMV report. But Fatal Insurance had no such rule, and therein lay its whole business plan in a nutshell: Fatal was not so cynical as to distrust its customers; no one was ever rejected, unless he was foolish enough to tell the truth on the application. Every customer thus walked out the door with a policy, and within a short while was behind the wheel, whether he was insurable or not. When a claim came in—and it seemed that customers with Fatal Insurance were invariably involved in accidents—the first thing we insurance adjusters would do was run a DMV report. If it turned out that the insured had been less than truthful on the application, this constituted a material misrepresentation, and thus voided the policy. Claim denied. Good-bye, have a nice day. And the premium, the policy's fine print made clear, was absolutely nonrefundable. The customer had engaged in fraud, after all; the company was the real victim here.

My time with Fatal Insurance, which is no longer in business, was brief, but the education in corporate predation was invaluable. Insurance companies, even relatively honest ones, can make their money only by denying claims.

HEALTH IS NOT PROPERLY INSURABLE, because everyone falls ill in time. No one is free of preexisting conditions; once we are born we begin to die. As people age, their complaints, conditions, aches, and afflictions multiply and the contradiction of health insurance becomes ever more untenable; thus the existence of Medicare, which is not insurance but a provision. As a society we *provide* health care to our elderly. Likewise, a rational system of national health care would not be an insurance system—it would be a provision, a common good paid for by the society as a whole. A mandatory insurance system, such as we have now, is merely an overcomplicated scheme to get healthy people to subsidize the care of unhealthy people—a perfectly reasonable public aim—while simultaneously pursuing the insane and unjustifiable private aim of funneling large profits to private corporations, which by their very nature will seek to maximize those profits by denying as many claims as possible.

A sign of what we face in our magnificent and historic new system appeared within a week of Obama's signing ceremony, as insurance companies let it be known that according to their reading of the health-care law and contrary to the much-publicized claims of the triumphant Democrats, insurers were not in fact required to cover children with preexisting conditions, because the law does not require companies to sell policies to people with preexisting conditions. If a company were to sell a particular family a policy, then it would have to cover a child in that family, even if the child suffered from leukemia. But the law does not yet force the company to sell a policy to that family, or so argued a lawyer by the name of William G. Schiffbauer, whose clients include insurance companies. That requirement does not come into effect until 2014, so if your child is dying of leukemia and you don't currently have insurance, or your insurer canceled your policy, or you've already hit the lifetime maximum, you'll just have to wait until then to get a policy. And don't be surprised if in 2014 the insurance companies have devised more loopholes to keep them from covering your dying child. Schiffbauer came up with his argument in less than week, and no doubt his colleagues at AHIP were soon cursing him, since Kathleen Sebelius, the secretary of health and human services, immediately shot off a letter warning that rules would soon be issued to prevent such perfectly sensible business decisions. The insurance industry backed down right quick, but no doubt future loopholes will be carefully husbanded during the next three years of full-court lobbying.

More than any other single political controversy in recent memory, the health-care debacle illustrates the brute fact that American political debate is largely carried on in the realm of fiction. The Democrats passed what is, in essence, a Republican health-care plan that does little more than tinker around the edges of the current failed system; the Republicans rejected the plan, refused to vote for it, denounced it as a socialist government takeover of a large sector of the economy—not because they were opposed to the plan in principle, but because they wished to deny the Democrats a legislative accomplishment. It was no doubt all the more galling that the legislation represented yet another Democratic appropriation of the Republican agenda, very much in the spirit of Bill Clinton's embrace of balancing the federal budget, passing NAFTA, and destroying Aid to Families with Dependent Children, an act of social vandalism also known as welfare reform. The Republicans' rejection was merely tactical. The debate was thus carried out in utter mendacity on both sides. What was really at stake was no more than party competition, temporary ascendency in the never-ending party war that was born in the early days of the republic.

Democrats believed they had to pass something, or they would face the midterm elections with nothing to show for a year's work. Republicans gambled that running against reform would play best in the midterm campaigns, that they would be able to shape public opinion in their favor no matter what the outcome. They were probably right; losses by the Democrats were almost certainly a given in a recessionary economy no matter what the outcome of the health-care battle, but opposition to the health-care bill gave the Republicans a very effective instrument to use in the campaign to shape public opinion to their advantage.

The stunning off-year election in Massachusetts, which resulted in Scott Brown's victory over Martha Coakley, the state attorney general and strong favorite, and the tragic loss of the Democrats' sixtieth Senate vote, had shown the way. Despite various rationalizations hazarded by the national Democratic Party and its apologists that the outcome was all Coakley's fault, large forces were clearly at work in that election. During the final weeks of the election significant contributions flowed into Brown's campaign from individuals employed in the finance industry—almost $450,000 in the week leading up to the election alone, with roughly 80 percent of the finance industry's funds coming from out of state. Moreover, 70 percent of all the donors to Brown's campaign from January 1 to January 19, 2010, came from out of state, compared with 8 percent in 2009. Brown also benefited from an extraordinary last-minute inflow of funds, which appeared to correspond with Obama's first experiments with anti-bank rhetoric, his talk of "fat-cat bankers," and so on. Political investors are nothing if not touchy; if you insult them too much they will fund your enemies. Brown had raised just over $1 million in 2009; between New Year's Day and the election on January 19, he raised more than $14 million. This was serious money. The national Republican Party had mobilized its donors to pull off a surprising coup, but clearly there was more going on in this election than brute money power. As Tom Ferguson and Jie Chen showed in a sensitive statistical analysis, the Democratic turnout in lower-income towns in Massachusetts was significantly depressed, and the results were directly correlated to unemployment levels and declines in housing prices.

The Democratic working-class base in Massachusetts simply did not turn out in January 2010. In a highly charged election, with motivated Republican donors determined to mobilize public opinion against controversial national legislation, a weak working-class turnout is a fatal result for Democrats. Since Massachusetts is one of the wealthier states and almost always goes Democratic, and is the state whose health-care system is the model for ObamaCare, the prospects for the Democrats in the 2010 midterm elections appeared very grim indeed. Poorer states tend to go Republican anyway, since lower-income people are less likely to vote and higher-income people in those states are much more likely to vote Republican. As of May 2010, unemployment rates remained very high all over the country—for example, in Michigan (14 percent), Nevada (13.7 percent), California (12.5 percent), and Rhode Island (12.5 percent). Black unemployment, nationwide, was at 16.5 percent. It's clear that the ongoing economic difficulties for middle- and lower-income people, even if it turns out that the economy is no longer officially in a recession, together with continued high unemployment and massive campaign spending by Republicans, augur a very bad congressional election cycle for Democrats.

The mechanics of the political business cycle are no mystery to policy makers, though the tools are somewhat crude and always subject to independent variables such as financial panics, economic depressions, wars, and perhaps even world-historical oil spills. It doesn't take a clairvoyant to see that the Bush business cycle peaked way too soon, and that if the bursting of the housing bubble and the subsequent panic hadn't come when they did, there is at least a chance we'd be puzzling over the antics of Vice President Palin. Political commentators of all stripes have wondered about the Obama administration's seemingly perverse insistence on attacking the health-care issue instead of pushing an extensive jobs program—Obama could presumably have used the apparently unlimited spending authority granted by the various bailout measures to put millions of people back to work very quickly, as FDR proved was possible during the first New Deal. Surely, it has been argued, such a plan might have improved the Democrats' chances in 2010. Of course the stimulus plan was backloaded to ensure that moneys would be disbursed in the months prior to the election, but there is much uncertainty about its potential effects. Such arguments also overlook the centrality of the *presidential* cycle. A big jobs bill early in Obama's term surely would have helped Democrats in Congress, but it might have peaked too soon to keep Obama in office in 2012. From the perspective of the White House, it would be far better to lose seats, even to lose a majority in the Senate, than for Barack Obama to be a one-term president. Besides, Obama no doubt had his eyes on his legacy. As his craven vice president had put it, his big white grin on high beam, Obama wanted be the One to achieve what no president had ever quite managed to do; he would sign national health care into law, even if it was a hollow sham.

CHAPTER SEVEN

RISE OF THE PSEUDO-CONS

American politics today displays a remarkable ideological incoherence. Since the rise of Ronald Reagan our public debates have been dominated by a rhetoric of conservatism and small government even as the standard-bearer of that ideology, the Republican Party, has increased government spending and the size of the federal bureaucracy, cut taxes on the rich, and waged war all across the globe, thus creating gargantuan federal budget deficits. A curious sort of conservatism it was that offered little in the way of conservation, preservation, or respect for tradition, and already in the 1980s figures such as John Lukacs had decisively debunked the Reaganites' conservative pretensions. The paradoxes of American pseudo-conservatism are endless; just Christian enough to hate their neighbors, they are likewise united in their hatred for liberals but show little evidence of being conservative enough to love liberty. Much was made of family values, but the economic policies embraced by the party offered little solace to struggling families of modest means working in the dying industries of the Midwest or the small farmers and ranchers whose lifeways were more and more under assault from the forces of globalization and agribusiness monopoly. Tax rates dropped, and so did most Americans' standard of living, while the richest 1 percent had not only more income but an ever-swelling share of national income. Epidemics of drugs and disease were met with indifference or worse; methamphetamines made a wasteland of rural America, and crack cocaine turned cities into war zones. Prison populations exploded. After the long years of steady postwar economic growth, the nineteenth-century laissez-faire cycle of boom and bust took hold again. Middle-class families played the stock market and lost everything, or speculated on real estate and lost everything. Yet the triumphal march of New Right pseudo-conservatism continued, with its voodoo doctrine of supply-side economics and racially tinged social science theories helping to explain the stubborn persistence of the so-called underclass.

Yet according to the conventional view of American politics that I absorbed as a young man in the 1980s, the modern Republican Party was the historical vehicle of wealth and patriotism. Democrats, at least the ones to be found in Washington, D.C., were untrustworthy, weak, and something less than real Americans. In Texas at that time, the Democratic Party was still dominant, but a Texas Democrat, it was understood, was an entirely different species from those simpering Yankees in places like Massachusetts and New York. I remember being struck with a sense of panic at the thought that President Reagan might be defeated by Walter Mondale. Most of my friends at Del Rio High School felt much the same way, and many of us were enthusiastic canvassers for the Republican ticket; I recall Reagan's reelection as being one of the happiest days of my adolescence. Today I cherish that memory as a demonstration of the enormous propagandizing power of the mass media.

Whatever it is that passes for political conservatism in the United States today, this curious hybrid ideology is not in any proper sense a disposition inclined to affection for traditional modes of life or, for that matter, any mode of life that does not thrive in a rudely destructive and abstract economy such as ours. No one who celebrates the creative destruction of laissez-faire capitalism, with its tearing asunder of all traditional ties, its reduction of all relationships to that of the cash transaction, should be considered a conservative in the proper sense—unless by conservative one means precisely the opposite. By today's incoherent standards even Edmund Burke himself would be derided as a bleeding heart, welfare-state socialist.

Although principled, authentic conservatives are not entirely extinct, the number of politicians capable of discussing the essays of, say, Michael Oakeshott is vanishingly small. In general, modern American conservatism—which is to say *movement* conservatism of the kind commonly demonstrated on Fox News and in the popular press—is a sad and degenerate descendent of the Old Right, a spendthrift cousin twice removed from the principled opponents of the New Deal, and is in its most quotidian manifestations an incoherent farrago of half-remembered revolutionary republican rhetoric, classical laissez-faire liberalism, Jacksonian nativism, Know-Nothing anti-intellectualism, and fundamentalist Christianity. United only by a jingo nationalism that would be comical if it were not so destructive, fragments of these wildly incompatible discourses cohabitate uneasily in pseudo-conservatism's shabby revivalist tent. The intellectual wing of the movement, often labeled neoconservatism, is somewhat more consistent but is better understood as hawkish neoliberalism, a capitalist mutation of the Trotskyite rage for permanent revolution joined with a fervent commitment to the divine righteousness of multinational corporations and uninhibited financial flows. Neoconservatism is an armed doctrine in search of a deregulated supply-side utopia.

At the level of party politics and everyday conversation, many of those who attempt to pass as liberals in our debased political culture are no better off than the pseudo-cons, terminologically or conceptually. Do our liberals follow Jeremy Bentham or John Stuart Mill, John Locke or John Rawls, Immanuel Kant or Jürgen Habermas? Are they classical liberals, procedural liberals, or human-rights liberals? Or are they old-fashioned New Dealers, devoted to Social Security, unemployment insurance, government regulation, and conservation of natural resources? Probably not the last-named, these days, since even our purportedly liberal president tells us that the New Deal is outmoded and that Social Security is far too expensive, because according to speculative (and spurious) projections it faces a funding crisis in thirty or forty years. "Liberalism," observed José Ortega y Gasset, "is the supreme form of generosity; it is the right which the majority concedes to minorities and hence it is the noblest cry that has ever resounded in this planet. It announces the determination to share existence with the enemy; more than that, with an enemy which is weak. It was incredible that the human species should have arrived at so noble an attitude, so paradoxical, so refined, so acrobatic, so anti-natural. Hence, it is not to be wondered at that this same humanity should soon appear anxious to get rid of it. It is a discipline too difficult and complex to take firm root on earth." Like conservatism, liberalism is more a disposition than an ideology, and properly understood is not even incompatible with conservatism. One might argue that our true conservatives today are the liberals who fight to preserve what is left of civil society, the public sphere, and our constitutional liberties from the depredations of privatizing neocons. In general, however, American liberals have been reduced to an embarrassing defensive cringe, a political attitude that dares not speak its name.

The common American liberal today, the kind of person you might actually have dinner with or talk to while watching your children play sports, is mostly interested in lifestyle— and the not inconsiderable virtues of tolerance, compassion, decency, and fair play. Lifestyle liberals tend to express the proper environmental pieties and feel very strongly about respecting the rights of racial, ethnic, and sexual minorities. All of these perfectly admirable liberal qualities and attitudes—all in keeping with Adam Smith's and David Hume's eighteenth-century advocacy of the civilizing and soothing effect of manners and politeness—are right, proper, and praiseworthy, but as modes of action and behavior they do not necessarily follow from a coherent political philosophy or a theory of government. American liberal philosophy does offer strong theories of distributive justice and rigorous decision procedures for determining whether actions are ethically and morally legitimate. Unfortunately, not many of these complex and brilliant theories translate very effectively into the languages of conflict and contestation within which energetic democratic debate, such as it is, takes place. They usually boil down—as in the public persona of Barack Obama—to variations on the very wise advice we received from our preschool teachers to be nice and gentle with one another. Consequently, in the field of political combat, such theories do not provide particularly effective weaponry against aggressive and well-financed corporate business interests.

Since the Reagan revolution the two broad streams of liberal-conservative workaday political confusion have superficially segregated themselves into the Democratic and Republican parties, the Republicans now decisively purged of the last remnants of their old progressive wing. The Democrats have managed no similar ideological purification—and in fact have tried very hard to shed their old New Deal associations, with the Blue Dogs and other proud centrists picking up the Dixiecrat banner, while the liberal base waits upon corrupt Wall Street barons like Charles Schumer, Chris Dodd, and Barney Frank. Such congeries of ideological, semantic, and philosophical doctrines amount to political misdirections more than anything else. During the thirty-odd years in which the New Deal system held sway, both parties broadly agreed on the tenets of the welfare state, and generally pursued a narrow competition characterized above all by foreign policy grandstanding. Thereafter, during the Reagan era, which alas we have not yet left behind, both parties generally agreed on the necessity of dismantling or at least starving the welfare state, despite its overwhelming popularity with the general public, and appeasing predatory and financially irresponsible corporations as they neglected, exported, and otherwise dismembered the greatest industrial infrastructure in world history. Both periods were marked by an almost unshakable consensus on national security and the necessity of commercial empire.

Obama and the current Democratic leadership represent the perfection of the long right turn the party took beginning in the 1970s. Although that trend had already begun during the Carter years, after Reagan's 1980 landslide it accelerated and a leading faction of the Democrats became convinced that only by shedding their association with the New Deal could they hope to compete with the Republicans for corporate patronage. After distancing themselves from the heritage of New Deal liberalism, however, Democrats were left with little to offer voters other than nerdy appeals to competence and sound management principles. That might work with corporate patrons, but voters were unimpressed. At the same time, for complex cultural reasons, the Democrats became convinced that the old style of cutthroat politics practiced with such consummate mastery by FDR and his protégé Lyndon Johnson, was somehow beneath them.

Thus emasculated, and shorn of their traditional programmatic means of attracting votes, the Democrats settled into a long decline, seemingly content to be the second-tier party. For some time, the Democrats' corporate patrons, preoccupied with low interest rates, free trade, and deficit reduction, were outgunned by the large Republican bloc, which was attracted by promises of enormous tax cuts, deregulation, and an ongoing decades-long military-industrial stimulus package. Bill Clinton, an enormously charismatic retail politician, took up the challenge of refashioning his party as a more efficient vehicle for business aspirations and slipped into office thanks to H. Ross Perot. Once in power, Clinton and his allies brazenly robbed Republicans of their most cherished objectives—passing NAFTA, gutting welfare programs, bombing Iraq—while somehow snookering the Democratic base into thinking Clinton was a progressive. Clinton's economic policies stimulated first the high-tech and dot-com bubble, then the housing bubble; and his repeal of New Deal–era safeguards such as Glass-Steagall set the stage for the financial crisis that brought on the Great Recession. Given the Democrats' career over the last three decades, it is difficult to avoid the conclusion that Democratic Party liberalism, overly stimulated by financial gimmickry, has committed suicide in a fit of autoerotic asphyxiation.

IF WE SET ASIDE THE semantics of liberalism and conservatism and glance back before the current party system, the true character of our politics is somewhat easier to grasp, though superficialities and propaganda often make clear judgments difficult. Historically, the contemporary Democratic Party is the decadent heir of Madison and Jefferson's opposition party, the mortal foe of Hamilton's Federalists. That original Republican party, founded on the support of agrarian interests, freeholders, and the rising class of business enterprise, in opposition to the mercantile powers of monarchism, debt financing, and securities speculation, eventually presided over the demise of the Federalists, the old party of oligarchy and consolidated energetic government—which, in a strange historical irony, perished in a New England secessionist orgy at the Hartford Convention of 1814. Within a few decades the Republicans themselves succumbed to intraparty warfare, with the followers of Andrew Jackson eventually assuming the epithet of Democracy, while Henry Clay and his faction eventually took up the old banner of the Whigs.

Out of the unnatural one-party calm of the Era of Good Feelings emerged a coalition of rising business interests that orbited the presidency of Andrew Jackson. The standard histories of this period narrate what is essentially a continuation of the battle between Federalists and Republicans, and certainly that is the flavor of the rhetoric. The great Bank War was the primary contest, though it seems that when Jackson arrived in Washington he had not yet set his mind on this path of glory. Many of Jackson's advisers were closely associated with state banks, and they seemed to have taken aim at the U.S. Bank early on. A brief glance at some of their business interests suggests why. Martin Van Buren, Jackson's vice president, was the former governor of New York and the creative spirit of the Albany Regency, as the New York political machine was known, and had very close ties to the New York banks. A master of the political dark arts, Van Buren worked to promote the economic interests of his home state, which quickly became the center of finance once the power of the U.S. Bank, based in Baltimore, was broken. Jackson's adviser and good friend Roger B. Taney, the future chief justice of the United States (and author of the Dred Scott decision), was a shareholder in the Union Bank of Baltimore and had a long involvement with banking. Amos Kendall, Jackson's postmaster general and political strategist, and the foremost member of the Kitchen Cabinet, was an extraordinary entrepreneur who gained control of Samuel Morse's patents and later founded the American Telegraph Company. Senator Thomas Hart Benton, a leading congressional Jacksonian associated with John Jacob Astor, had been a stockholder in the Bank of Saint Louis and the director of the Bank of Missouri, which closed in 1821, apparently because of pressure from the Kentucky branch of the federal bank, so perhaps he had a personal grudge as well. All these men were aggressive political and business entrepreneurs whose friends and associates saw centralized finance as an obstacle to their ambitions.

Aside from their republican and populist rhetoric about the evils of the moneyed interests, there was nothing particularly agrarian about the Jacksonians' attack—they did not assail corporations, corporate rights, property, wealth, or capitalism but were in fact developing a new, more modern, perhaps more democratic, but certainly more vigorous and eventually more predatory version of the corporation. When Jackson and Taney removed federal deposits from the U.S. Bank in 1833 they simply put the moneys into their own pet state banks. They created a system of unregulated state-bank paper currency that contributed, no doubt against their conscious wishes, to continued cycles of boom and bust, expansion and depression. Free banking was simply an excellent way to make money, very fast, without regard to broader economic ramifications. Although bankruptcy legislation was enacted, and Martin Van Buren worked to abolish debtors' prisons, in general the Jacksonians did not believe in helping the working people who suffered so terribly during the increasingly frequent financial panics and depressions that resulted from destroying the U.S. Bank. Minimum wage legislation, unemployment relief, the ten-hour workday, and other labor reforms all failed. Andrew Jackson even innovated by using federal troops to break a strike. Jackson and Van Buren saw their greatest successes in the invention of new techniques of mobilizing public opinion and turning out voters. Jacksonian Democracy gave birth to the modern political machine.

Hamiltonian Federalism, meanwhile, had hidden itself in Whiggery, and once purged of the old silk-stocking, gentlemanly rhetoric, it adopted a strategy of evasion and disguise, increasingly adopting the jargon of Jacksonian democratic authenticity. Gone were the old candid invocations of property and moneyed responsibility and the necessity of binding the rich to government. Politicians were not interested in power or money—they spoke only of free speech, a free press, education, internal improvements, liberty, justice, the Constitution, Union, God, and sweet mothers everywhere. The Whigs were no less corrupt than the Jacksonians, as Daniel Webster's famous note to Nicholas Biddle, the president of the U.S. Bank, makes clear. Webster's candor was magnificent: "I believe my retainer has not been renewed or *refreshed* as usual," he wrote to Biddle. "If it be wished that my relation to the Bank should be continued, it may be well to send me the usual retainers." When it did take power, the Whig Party, like the Federalists, became the party of commercial empire, in contrast to the Democrats' mania for continental expansion and Indian wars. It was under the Whigs that relations were established with China in 1844 and, ten years later, Commodore Perry forced China to open its doors to American trade. The third Republican Party, successor to the Whigs and Federalists, political vehicle of the railroad interests, defeated the slave power, and by the end of the Civil War and Reconstruction it had reestablished many of the old Federalist positions, particularly the national debt, the protective tariff, a federal bank to regulate the currency, and the pursuit of overseas commercial empire. Although William H. Seward, as secretary of state in the 1860s, tried mightily to pursue a large strategy internationally—declaring that Canada should be annexed as well as Mexico and other Latin American republics; that the Pacific would be the new frontier; that America and Russia would meet in battle on the plains of Asia—it took William McKinley to bring the American empire into its full flower overseas.

During the post–Civil War years of GOP supremacy, when the party was captured by mercenaries and spoilsmen of every conceivable description, the Democrats began their long march to redemption. Minor parties and insurgents rose up from time to time, and though they were usually captured by one of the major parties they did manage to transform or at least modify the two dominant party platforms and see some of their concerns represented in law. Thus the old working-men's groups, active as far back as the 1830s, gave way to the labor reformers, the Socialists, and the American Federation of Labor; independent agrarian societies sprang up, calling themselves Granges, the Greenback Party, and the Farmers Alliance, and came together in the Populist Party, which the Democrats (backed by Anaconda, Hearst, and the silver interests) with diabolical skill neutralized and absorbed.

As the agitators rose up and passed away, Jeffersonian rhetoric was a continual inspiration, even if the party of the great Virginian was a continual disappointment. Aristocracy, plutocracy, oligarchy, exploitation of the farmer and the workingman—these things have remained a constant in our history. Both the Populists and the Progressives made many of the old agrarian demands—free coinage of silver and other schemes for even easier money, lower tariffs to keep the prices of consumer goods low for working people, busting of trusts and the other artificial leviathans of the moneyed interests, loans to farmers, regulation of the railroads, shorter work-weeks and workdays. Even so, the Hamiltonian system proved resilient and capable of assimilating all opposition. After the election of 1896 came the mercenary machine politics of Mark Hanna and William McKinley, backed by J. P. Morgan, along with imperialism, the annexation of Hawaii, war with

Spain, and the annexation of Puerto Rico, Guam, and the Philippines. The political crisis of the 1890s had the perverse effect of inspiring McKinley's large policy of imperial conquest, which demonstrated to clever politicians of whichever party that the old political insight that foreign wars are always useful for distracting an unruly and discontented domestic populace was fully applicable in the United States. McKinley, however, made do with relatively small wars against weak adversaries, spending a negligible amount of American blood and treasure—and the wars, at least by later standards, were not expanded beyond the minimum. Despite the gory ambitions of jingoes like Theodore Roosevelt and the expansion of America's commercial empire in the Pacific, the elaboration of the Open Door Policy, the damage to republican institutions was not necessarily fatal. But the precedent had been set, and men of boundless ambition had taken note.

The platform of the Democratic Party in 1900 denounced the "greedy commercialism which dictated the Philippine policy of the Republican administration" and "the war of criminal aggression against the Filipinos." Certain truths were held to be self-evident, including the axiom that the Constitution follows the flag. "We assert that no nation can long endure half republic and half empire, and we warn the American people that imperialism abroad will lead quickly and inevitably to despotism at home." Even after McKinley's assassination at the hands of an anarchist, by 1912 not much had changed in the Democratic Party's official position: "We condemn the experiment in imperialism as an inexcusable blunder." Yet such laudable pieties did nothing to prevent America's messianic adventures in the twentieth century. When Theodore Roosevelt abandoned his formerly reluctant and highly selective approach to trust-busting and walked out of the Republican Party, declaring that the old parties were both "tools of the corrupt interests" he thereby demonstrated that the backing of those interests was yet a condition of national political success. As leader of the new Progressive Party, he vowed "to dissolve the unholy alliance between corrupt business and corrupt politics." Declaring that "the government of the United States at present is a foster child of the special interests," Roosevelt promised to make war on "the big bankers, the big manufacturers, the big masters of commerce, the heads of railroad corporations and the steamship corporations."

Thus he more or less handed the election to Woodrow Wilson, an uncommonly eloquent and ambitious academic whose theoretical preference for an imperial presidency, coupled with his personal vainglory and his moralistic ambition to teach the world to live according to American prejudices, led the nation into the Great War. Wilson was an old-fashioned Democrat who believed in states' rights, white supremacy, laissez-faire, and minimal government, yet he aligned himself with the progressives—many of whom in fact subscribed to the pseudoscientific racism of the day. Wilson had contempt for the Declaration of Independence and the Constitution and believed that the evolution of government made a supremely powerful executive inevitable. In order to be the great leader that he had always dreamed of becoming, Wilson knew he would have to embark on an energetic foreign policy.

National greatness for Wilson could be understood only in terms of presidential greatness.

Historical analogies and comparisons between Barack Obama and his various predecessors have become routine, even a journalistic cliché, but they are irresistible. Immediately after the 2008 election there were many comparisons between Obama and Franklin Roosevelt; by the summer of 2009 it was clear that Herbert Hoover was a better model. Obama, unlike Roosevelt, was not a bold innovator willing to hazard his political fortunes on radical reinventions of policy. He was instead a timid follower of political convention. After Obama's recent Washington surge (the appalling insurance bailout, the long slow comical finance reform variety show), loose and irresponsible comparisons to LBJ have begun to slip into our newspapers and blogs of record. But in many respects Wilson provides an even more revealing historical precedent and parallel—a Democrat coming into office after a long Republican ascendency marked by aggressive military adventurism and the establishment of an overseas empire. Wilson, despite the progressive rhetoric of the New Freedom, was essentially a stand-pat conservative, a great admirer of corporations and businessmen who was happy to provide the financiers, the holding companies, and the trusts with what they needed: new laws to legitimize their business activities and protect them not only from the public but from competitors that would be disadvantaged by regulatory expenses. Wilson, like Obama a sometime academic, a man of considerable intellect and rhetorical facility, came into power riding a wave of popular disgust and reformist energy, which he exploited adroitly, even brilliantly, and which he then proceeded to betray systematically, tossing his ideals and promises overboard just as soon as he was safely elected.

Wilson's reforms did nothing to prevent the entrenchment of the corporation, which was eventually helped along by the Supreme Court's arbitrary extension of the rights of personhood to private corporations in 1886, as the predominant center of power in the American political economy. Robert La Follette called the Federal Reserve Act a "big bankers' bill," and it was in fact the culmination of a long campaign by bankers such as Paul Warburg of Kuhn, Loeb to establish a central bank in the United States. The act gave business what it needed and appeased public fury, leaving the balance of economic power unchanged.

Wilson's reformist accomplishments pale in comparison with his pernicious messianic ambitions and puritanical zeal to make the world safe for democracy. With the closing of the frontier and the exhaustion of continental expansion, dangerous imperial tendencies that had manifested themselves throughout the nineteenth century culminated in a forced march into World War I and the repressive police state enabled by the Espionage Act and the Sedition Act of 1918, with A. Mitchell Palmer's spies and thugs scouring the land for Reds to deport and pacifists to imprison. Between the wars the police state relaxed; Harding and Coolidge rolled back Wilson's taxes and moved the Federal Reserve to the right; and the commercial empire continued its expansion in spite of the weirdly persistent myth of isolationism. The Democrats lost touch with what remained of their agrarian roots, though they retained some of the old rhetoric, and became increasingly an urban party, a party of the new immigrants. Hoover, a man of great accomplishments, perhaps the most distinguished presidential candidate of the twentieth century, lived by business and died by the business cycle. Franklin Roosevelt, a masterful political tactician and charming patrician trimmer, had no illusions about the wisdom of businessmen and was clever enough to surround himself with men and women of sufficient vision and energy to improvise themselves out of a catastrophe. To our great good fortune, Roosevelt and his famous Brains Trust bequeathed to subsequent generations a modest if flawed social safety net, an inheritance that our current rulers are determined to squander. The productive boom of Roosevelt's war mobilization, coupled with sound principles for the regulation of the economy, propelled the United States through a period of unequaled prosperity.

Both parties represented the varying agendas of either the moneyed establishment or rising upstarts and enterprisers who wished to take the establishment's place. Republicans alternated in power with the Democrats, trading off successive waves of reaction and progressivism, protection and free trade, isolation and imperialism. Each party toyed with reform as necessary to soothe the savage voters in their periodic uprisings against plutocracy or economic depression, and enriched its backers as a matter of course. Most significantly, of course, the New Deal finally enshrined in law a broad raft of social programs that had been the objective of popular agitation for decades. Tragically, Roosevelt's presidency also represents the moment when the United States decisively crossed the Rubicon into global empire. Contrary to the assertions of right-wing publicists, it was not the New Deal that destroyed what remained of the old republic but the cataclysm of World War II, which called forth a total mobilization of our society for the purpose of war that never ended. Truman's launch of the Cold War set us on a permanent war footing, and since then no president of either party—not Kennedy or Johnson, and certainly not Nixon, Ford, or Carter, who began the arms race that Reagan accelerated—has challenged the assumptions of the national security state.

The Cold War and its jealous safeguarding of American hegemony once was justified in terms of the open society and its enemies; our most learned and clever international strategists claimed that communism must be contained lest the United States become a liberal democratic island, surrounded by a dangerous sea of illiberal enemies. No open society can survive such encirclement, they argued, and America would in that situation inevitably devolve into a garrison state. All our liberties would be sacrificed one by one. Thus it was necessary, for the national interest, to use illiberal means abroad to protect liberal government at home. Noble lies must be employed, and good men must sacrifice their conscience and do evil in the name of a greater good. Covert operations, assassinations, proxy wars, limited invasions, coups, and alliances with dictators and killers of every description ensued. Over time the old rationalizations were mostly forgotten, and by the time communism collapsed under the weight of its internal contradictions, the maintenance of American empire had assumed a logic all its own, severed from its early idealistic dependence on the preservation of domestic liberty. The business of empire looked for new markets, and September 11 provided a perfect opportunity to apply Milton Friedman's dictum that no crisis should ever be wasted.

As Madison wrote in 1795, "Of all the enemies to public liberty, war is, perhaps, the most to be dreaded, because it comprises and develops the germ of every other. War is the parent of armies; from these proceed debts and taxes; and armies, and debts, and taxes are the known instruments for bringing the many under the domination of the few. In war, too, the discretionary power of the Executive is extended; its influence in dealing out offices, honors, and emoluments is multiplied; and all the means of seducing the minds are added to those of subduing the force of the people. The same malignant aspect in republicanism may be traced in the inequality of fortunes and the opportunities of fraud growing out of a state of war, and in the degeneracy of manners and of morals engendered by both. No nation could reserve its freedom in the midst of continual warfare." The national security state put the immortal national debt to the very purpose that had so haunted good republicans from Thomas Gordon to Thomas Jefferson: a vast and permanent military establishment that through its influence and malignant power has fatally distorted our constitutional balance.

CHAPTER EIGHT

THE LONG EMERGENCY

To point out that the eighteenth-century republicans were right to fear the codependency of national debt and a permanent standing army is not to indulge in preposterous nostalgia for a citizen militia; the necessity of a permanent and professional military has been a foregone conclusion since the Jefferson administration. Nor is it even meant to question the modern necessity of responsible debt financing, especially of emergency measures, whether military or economic. After all, the United States has run a national debt for its entire history, except for a brief period in the mid–1830s, and there's an excellent argument that deficits are economically beneficial— and that significant and sudden reductions in the national debt seem to correspond with economic depressions. The analogy between a national economy and a household is not only flawed but dangerously flawed. Modern deficit hawks have retained the hatred for national debt but not the fear of a politically powerful military establishment that historically has always contributed to the death of republican government.

There could be no more dramatic example of such perils than the vast military establishment of the United States, with its nearly 1,000 foreign military bases, 5,000 nuclear weapons, and more than 2 million personnel. Since the end of World War II, the United States has maintained the largest and most powerful war machine in world history. Military spending, according to the official figures, consumes more than 22 percent of all federal spending, but many expenses that are intimately tied to the war machine, such as the Department of Homeland Security, nuclear weapons, and spending on veterans, are hidden in other parts of the budget. The military swallows well over 50 percent of the discretionary budget, and calculations by independent analysts suggest that the true proportion of the overall federal budget that is devoted to war is between 44 and 54 percent. In 2001, the U.S. defense budget was $296 billion; by 2009 it had increased 73 percent to $513 billion. The 2010 Pentagon budget is more than $636 billion. The wars in Iraq and Afghanistan, which have largely been funded outside the base military budget, add more than $1 trillion in military spending and will probably cost trillions more. Actual spending on the military in 2009 was estimated to be about $721 billion; it was projected to be $728 billion in 2010 and $737 billion in 2011. As numerous critics of American militarism have argued, we do not really have a defense *budget* in the United States; our presidential emperor simply spends whatever he wishes, and Congress just writes the checks. Terrorists, however, whether they are militant Islamists or antiabortion Christians, have no need of debt financing. Iraqi insurgents can build an IED and destroy a $100,000 Humvee for about the cost of a pizza. Small quantities of plastic explosives can bring down airplanes with ease. Likewise, car bombs are cheap and relatively uncomplicated. Roughly a dozen highly incompetent and unimpressive aspirational terrorists have attempted to attack New York since 2001, all foiled by basic police work or by their own manifest idiocy. For such threats, we need a $700 billion military? Our 250,000 soldiers in Iraq and Afghanistan—and at least that many mercenaries—can do precisely nothing to prevent a Nigerian underwear bomber from expressing his hatred for our goodness. And there is no foreseeable *military* threat—as opposed to the essentially *criminal* threat of hijackers and car bombers—to the United States that could not be met with a realistic military budget half the size of the current bloated monstrosity. All our war machine does is seed the world with enemies; every Predator drone that kills a dozen women and children in Pakistan thereby increases the likelihood of a Times Square fertilizer bomb.

The power nexus created during the Cold War by the merger of corporate and military power, denounced famously by Dwight D. Eisenhower in his farewell address as the military-industrial complex and lucidly described by C. Wright Mills in his 1956 masterpiece *The Power Elite*, is a vast imperial cancer that has grown larger than its republican host. Party competition is nonexistent when it comes to defense spending, because everyone in both parties profits from the campaign contributions, the bases, and the other spending duly apportioned across the fifty states. A whole intellectual support network has grown up, as if by hydroponics, in the well-funded think tanks across the nation whose primary purpose often seems to be the provision of intellectual justifications for ever more irresponsible militarism. Even so, in the absence of any credible threat, by the late 1990s defense spending had gradually declined to about 17 percent of federal outlays and 3.5 percent of GDP, much to the frustration of neoconservative agitators such as Donald Rumsfeld, Paul Wolfowitz, Richard Perle, and Dick Cheney. Even then it was too big, but the danger posed to the American war machine by the collapse of communism was lifted with the timely and convenient assistance of Osama bin Laden, and for a time it seemed that the press and a gullible public would permit the "long war" to continue forever and ever without end.

Happily for those who dream of experiencing constitutional governance in the United States (but not so happily for those who were tortured), the Bushites were greedy and unnecessarily thuggish; they overreached and provoked the courts and the press, and by the time of Barack Obama's inspiring change–hope triumph in 2008 a small library's worth of books decrying the imperialism and tyranny of the Bush administration had been published. Such oppositional tracts have mostly ceased to appear, at least on the left, yet the constitutional crisis that was brought about by George W. Bush's assertion of absolute power has not passed. As president,

Obama has held on to most of the Bushite powers; and the doctrine of the unitary executive, a partial-birth abortion of the Constitution assisted by Supreme Court Justice Samuel Alito when he worked in Reagan's Justice Department, no matter how many times it has been demolished and discredited by able legal scholars, continues to exert influence. The theory holds, in sum, that whatever the president does is legal. Under Reagan, the theory was used to justify the president's violation of the Boland Amendment, which prohibited military aid to the contras in their long war to overthrow the democratically elected Sandinista government of Nicaragua. Reagan's lawyers held that the Boland Amendment was an unconstitutional infringement of the president's sole and absolute authority over foreign affairs. The argument for such authority was based more on a dubious understanding of the inherent nature of executive power than on a close reading of the Constitution or of the debates surrounding its ratification. Few outside the administration and its immediate circle of journalistic and think-tank courtiers were convinced. These constitutional fictions nevertheless prepared the way for the Iran-contra affair, an exuberant carnival of felonious activity that should have led to an impeachment trial—but that would have required a true opposition party, and the bipartisan consensus in Washington was unwilling to risk shattering the general public's confidence in the system. Impeachment would have to await Oval Office fellatio.

Reagan's lawyers argued that the president by inherent right exercised total and complete administrative control over executive-branch agencies. Such arguments, though they drew on vigorous debates between Hamilton and Madison in the 1790s, were a radical departure from our constitutional tradition of congressional oversight; and in cases before the Supreme Court in which such arguments were presented they received little sympathy. In *Morrison v. Olson*, the administration attempted to challenge the legality of the Ethics in Government Act, which provided for an independent counsel whom the president would have difficulty removing if an investigation proved inconvenient. Theodore Olson, an assistant U.S. attorney in the Justice Department's Office of Legal Counsel, had argued that the president possesses an absolute prerogative over members of the executive branch and that he was thus permitted to fire anyone for any reason. The separation of powers, so interpreted, was absolute, and given the enormous scope of the executive branch's jurisdiction in modern life, the theory of the unitary executive has the effect of making the president an elected monarch. Not even Chief Justice William Rehnquist would go that far; he wrote in the majority (7-1) decision that "this rigid demarcation—a demarcation incapable of being altered by law in the slightest degree, and applicable to tens of thousands of holders offices neither known nor foreseen by the framers—depends upon an extrapolation from general constitutional language which we think is more than the text will bear." Only Justice Antonin Scalia accepted the theory.

After the attacks of September 11, the Bush administration seized the opportunity provided by the emergency to make an even more radical play for unitary dominion over all aspects of presidential authority, especially with regard to presidential war powers. Congress, as usual looking more toward temporary political expediency than constitutional principle, mostly went along, passing a vague authorization to use military force that the administration cited to justify its broad assertions of power. But it was in reaction to the discovery of Bush's secret torture program—the unilateral suspension of the writ of habeas corpus and establishment of a secret network of torture prisons overseas to hide his activities from the courts—that the unitary-executive assertions came most dramatically into play. Challenged with clear evidence of illegal torture and other war crimes prohibited by United States law and by treaty law, especially by the Geneva Conventions and the Convention against Torture, the administration defiantly claimed that the law did not apply, that the president and his advisers were within their rights as the sole authority over matters of war and foreign relations to reinterpret treaties and declare them inoperative or to declare that terrorists, as "unlawful combatants," were not covered by those laws. It was asserted that the president could make his own judgment that an individual was in fact a terrorist or an unlawful combatant and thus could be imprisoned without hope of appeal. On the basis of the president's—or, more often, the vice president's—arbitrary and unchecked judgment, moreover, an individual could be put to torture. Indeed, when asked whether the president was legally entitled to order that a child's testicles be crushed, John Yoo, the Justice Department's attorney who authored the most notorious memos justifying torture, replied, "I think it depends on why the president thinks he needs to do that."

There's little doubt that Bush, Cheney, and their partners in crime were scared. They were terrified that another attack was coming and that they would be blamed. But cowardice is no defense of outright felonies, especially the high crime of violating the Constitution and violating the clear language of congressional statute, and there is no doubt that by choosing to treat the atrocities of a criminal gang as acts of war, the administration's wise men were able to usurp powers they had long coveted. The Bush administration was following a well-worn historical path, suspending the Constitution and assuming dictatorial powers as Adams, Lincoln, and Wilson had done, but this time in an emergency that was explicitly described as permanent.

Public opinion and the press offered little resistance, but fortunately the law is a conservative institution in the best sense of that term, and principled lawyers—from academia, the ACLU, and the Center for Constitutional Rights, as well as attorneys in private practice who took on the cases pro bono—immediately went to work defending the victims of torture and illegal detention. After years of litigation, cases began to appear before the Supreme Court, and once again the Constitution was saved from the tyranny—this is the precise and technical term—of the unitary executive by our court of final appeal. The Supreme Court decided, for example—in *Rasul v. Bush* and in *Hamdi v. Rumsfeld*—that prisoners, both foreign nationals and U.S. citizens, held at Guantánamo Bay Naval Base do in fact have the right to challenge their detention with habeas corpus petitions in the civilian court system. Two years later, in *Hamdan v. Rumsfeld*, the court held that the military commissions set up by the Bush administration were illegal. Indeed, even a child could see that the president's decision to institute military commissions for such prisoners was clearly an attempt to avoid judicial oversight, as well as an attempt to avoid further embarrassing revelations about American torture policies. Congress, however, passed the Military Commissions Act of 2006, which attempted to strip the prisoners at Guantánamo of their right of habeas corpus. In 2008, in *Boumediene v. Bush*, the Court once again rebuked the administration and reasserted its jurisdiction over the prisoners.

Bush's practice of attaching "signing statements" to laws, a practice also pioneered by the Reagan administration, was another manifestation of the unitary-executive doctrine. Bush was much more aggressive than Reagan had been, using signing statements to nullify 1,200 legislative items during his two terms, twice the total number challenged by every other president in history combined. By setting forth an interpretation of the new statute and indicating which portions the executive would not be enforcing—out of constitutional scruples, of course—the president thus usurped not only legislative power but judicial power as well. Such signing statements are essentially line-item vetos. Bush and his subordinates also claimed the right, under their expansive theory of presidential war powers, to spy on Americans illegally, without search warrants, in direct defiance of congressional statute. As the inevitable legal challenges arose, an expansive doctrine of state secrets was put forth to shield the administration's high crimes and misdemeanors from public view, and this dubious state-secrets argument was employed to hamper the civil lawsuits of torture victims and others whose lives were shattered by American lawlessness. Moreover, the Justice Department itself was transformed into an instrument of partisan politics as Democratic politicians were targeted for prosecution during election cycles, and one former Democratic governor was convicted in highly irregular circumstances and imprisoned.

When the Archangel Obama was campaigning for president, he was severely critical of the unitary-executive doctrine, and he has been careful as president to make no appeals to it. As a candidate he promised to end torture, end the war in Iraq, and restore the dignity and moral stature of the United States. On August 1, 2007, in an address at the Wilson Center in Washington, in the most eloquent terms, he denounced the use of military commissions. He pointed out that there had been (up to that point) only one conviction at Guantánamo and it was not even for a terrorist act. He proclaimed his faith in America's courts. "As president," he said, "I will close Guantánamo, reject the Military Commissions Act, and adhere to the Geneva Conventions." In one of his first acts as president, Obama signed a series of executive orders banning the use of waterboarding, one of the more egregious and indefensible of the Bushite "enhanced interrogation techniques." He ordered the closing of the Guantánamo Bay concentration camp within a year. He ordered the closing of the CIA's network of black sites—secret prisons where alleged terrorists were held and tortured, hidden from judicial oversight and the Red Cross. He promised to make government transparent and accountable, and he nominated a prominent critic of Bush's Justice Department, Dawn Johnsen, to head the Office of Legal Counsel (OLC), the Justice Department office that had been responsible for the illegal and discredited torture memos of John Yoo and others. Johnsen, who worked in the OLC for five years before heading it in 1997–1998, had written eloquently of the need to restore the rule of law and prosecute those who had subverted the constitution: "We must avoid any temptation simply to move on," she wrote in 2008. "We must instead be honest with ourselves and the world as we condemn our nation's past transgressions and reject Bush's corruption of our American ideals. Our constitutional democracy cannot survive with a government shrouded in secrecy, nor can our nation's honor be restored without full disclosure." Civil libertarians were ecstatic.

Not for long. Soon it was admitted by Leon Panetta, Obama's nominee for CIA director, that extraordinary renditions, the practice of abducting individuals and then rendering them to a foreign government, would continue, but only if the United States received assurances that the kidnapped persons—who had been accused, tried, and sentenced by executive fiat—would not be tortured. Surely the Egyptians wouldn't lie about something like torture. There was a brief frenzy of hand-wringing among civil-liberties activists, but many comforted themselves with the thought that perhaps Panetta was simply trying to get through the confirmation hearing. Maybe he didn't really mean it. After the Obama administration released a set of the Bush Justice Department's torture memos, demands increased for criminal and civil sanctions against attorneys such as John Yoo and others who created the torture program. The uproar encouraged attacks

THE MENDACITY OF HOPE

from Dick Cheney and his army of surrogates, and Obama and his own political wise men seem to have panicked, fearing that transparency, accountability, and the rule of law were going too far. National honor be damned; they might derail the president's very important agenda, like bailing out the banks and big pharma and the health insurance industry. Constitutional governance and the rule of law would have to wait. There would be no more releases of horrifying memos or abuse photos, no more accountability. And, as he had repeatedly promised to do during the campaign, Obama quietly sent 21,000 more troops to Afghanistan.

By the time Obama took office, however, it was far from clear why we should continue to send our soldiers there to die. Candidate Obama, whether out of sincere belief or cynical opportunism, had attacked the Bush administration for abandoning the right and just war in Afghanistan in order to pursue its dreams of Middle East hegemony in Iraq. But the enormity of the September 11 attacks and the continuing insult of Osama bin Laden's existence were apparently enough to justify a new escalation in Afghanistan. The problem was that Al Qaeda, which in many ways resembles an innovative transnational corporation, had moved its headquarters to a more hospitable country; top executives were telecommuting from remote locations, and most of its operations had been outsourced to contractors and subsidiaries in places like Yemen or Somalia. Intelligence estimates put the number of Al Qaeda operatives in Afghanistan at fewer than 100. In fact, we no longer hear very much about Al Qaeda in connection with Afghanistan, because our prime adversary there is

the Taliban, a native Islamist movement that has been transformed by our occupation into a struggle for national liberation. Yet the new president continued to parrot the tired
phrases of the Bush administration about denying Al Qaeda a
safe haven and, despite the illegitimacy and corruption of the
Karzai regime, creating a stable and democratic government
in Kabul.

If the rationale for the war had been lost, and also the
definition of victory, it followed by an iron law of military
necessity that questions of strategy and tactics would become muddled as well. How shall we achieve victory if we
no longer know what victory would be? The old science-
fiction claims of the 1990s and early 2000s that America's
full-spectrum dominance and scalpel-like precision targeting
had created a revolution in military affairs have been revealed
to be as empty as Wall Street's advertisements for the benefits
of financial innovation. Instead, we are back to the old boots-
on-the-ground village-to-village and house-to-house warfare
of Vietnam (or even of the Philippines). The Pentagon has
deployed anthropologists to help the army's so-called human-
terrain teams persuade Afghan civilians that the Americans
are really there to help, and top generals like David Petraeus
and Stanley McChrystal have mused publicly that victory in
Afghanistan depends on politics and nation building rather
than military supremacy, yet with fateful regularity, night-
time raids by McChrystal's Special Forces continue to result
in the slaughter of noncombatants, children, and pregnant
women.

On December 1, 2009, after a long and highly publicized

reevaluation of his policy in Afghanistan—a policy review punctuated by the leak of a report by McChrystal warning of "mission failure" if more troops were not provided—Obama delivered a speech at West Point to announce his new plan to win the war. The setting was imperial. Before an audience of cadets who had devoted their young lives to the service of the state stood their commander in chief, a man sworn to defend the Constitution of the United States, who held their futures in his gentle palms. He stepped forward and to the world's astonishment gave a performance that can only be described as Nixonian. In addition to the 21,000 troops he had already sent to Afghanistan, he would send another 30,000 in an absurd one-year surge, after which they would immediately begin to withdraw—to initiate, in Obama's ludicrous formulation, the "transition to Afghan responsibility." It was obvious that the Archangel was slightly ill at ease in the imperial trappings, yet he did his best, lying to the young cadets and the American people as if his presidency depended on it. Perhaps he believed that it did. He did not explain how he knew that the surge would achieve its objectives within one year; he did not explain how defeating the Taliban in Afghanistan would end Al Qaeda's ability to operate in Pakistan; he did not explain how even the absolute and total conquest of Afghanistan would prevent new terrorist attacks in United States. He did, however, ring the familiar changes on the old tunes of American patriotism. He asserted that America, "unlike the great powers of old," has not sought world domination, and he sounded hurt that "we have not always been thanked" for spilling "American blood in many countries on multiple continents."

It was a curious moment, because during the campaign Obama had been consistently hawkish about Afghanistan, yet for many liberals it represented a complete repudiation of everything that he had stood for as a candidate. It seems that his antiwar supporters simply had not believed that their heroic candidate would keep fighting such a senseless war. The soaring rhetoric of hope and change was now replaced with the tired clichés of American exceptionalism, which eight years of Bush–Cheney misrule have permanently refuted. Not everyone was dismayed by the speech, of course; Hendrik Hertzberg of the *New Yorker* described it as "a sombre appeal to reason," and Frank Rich, unwavering in his adjectival devotion, asserted in the *New York Times* that the speech was "the sincere product of serious deliberations, an earnest attempt to apply his formidable intelligence to one of the most daunting Rubik's Cubes of foreign policy America has ever known."

All great powers justify their wars with noble sentiments. The logic of empire is domination, and the logic of war is killing; it is folly to pretend otherwise. The history of insurgent wars against imperial invaders is eloquent in its unanimity: the war will not end until the invaders leave. Shortly after the speech, anonymous sources reassured hawkish journalists and intellectuals that the president's talk of withdrawal shouldn't be taken *literally*, that facts on the ground would dictate all decisions. Even worse, analogies with our multigenerational presence in Europe in the aftermath of World War II began to proliferate. If we leave Afghanistan, Obama's courtiers whispered in the press, Pakistan and India will be consumed in a nuclear holocaust. America remains the indispensable nation.

Back in the land of the free, lawyers at the Justice Department were asserting the Bushite state-secrets defense in lawsuits regarding illegal surveillance. Likewise, state-secrets doctrine was evoked in lawsuits brought by victims of rendition and torture (victims who happened to be entirely innocent of any connection to terrorism). For example, in the case of Binyam Mohamed, a British citizen who was wrongfully arrested in Pakistan, rendered, severely tortured under the supervision of the CIA, and then held in Guantánamo for six years, the Obama administration tried to impose its curious theories about justice on the British government. Mohamed had sued for damages in a British court, which ruled against the Labour government, deciding that evidence of his torture—which included slicing his genitals with a scalpel—could not be suppressed for reasons of national security. Secretary of State Hillary Clinton threatened to withhold intelligence regarding suspected terrorists, in an effort to force the British government to comply with its policy of impunity. More perniciously, Obama's Justice Department deployed the constitutionally dubious doctrine of "sovereign immunity" in an attempt to dismiss surveillance lawsuits. Sovereign immunity is a common-law legal concept, derived from the monarchical axiom that the king can do no wrong, and it has a long history in American jurisprudence, though scholars have denounced it as alien to our republican form of government. Obama's use of the concept in the surveillance cases is particularly disturbing, since the Bush administration's illegal surveillance was in clear violation of the FISA statute, which thus should rule out the claim of sovereign immunity. According to the logic of

Obama's argument, the United States government cannot be held liable for illegal surveillance under any circumstances at all—not merely because such lawsuits would reveal state secrets, but because the government is *immune* from the people's claims by virtue of its *sovereignty*.

In all these cases, the overriding concern of the Obama administration is to suppress evidence of American criminal behavior so as to avoid further lawsuits and to appease the national security establishment. It is also clear that Obama's stance goes beyond cowardly avoidance of political conflict; he has embraced those policies and made them his own. Leon Panetta, director of the CIA, admitted that he would ask for authority to torture a suspected terrorist to prevent an imminent attack, thereby tacitly affirming, despite his denials, the Bushite assertion that the president as the unitary executive may suspend laws at will. Obama repeatedly threatened to veto the 2010 Intelligence Authorization Bill; in terms that conspicuously echoed the Bush administration, he cited encroachments on executive authority that would result from modest congressional oversight of covert operations. When Congress was considering the renewal of the Patriot Act in the fall of 2009, the Obama administration sided with Republicans to remove protections of civil liberties that had been included in the new bill; in February 2010, in a voice vote, without debate, the Senate voted to renew the Patriot Act with all its abusive powers left intact. The House quietly followed a few days later.

On the day before Obama nominated Elena Kagan to be his stealth candidate to replace John Paul Stevens, Attorney

General Eric Holder proposed a terrorism exception to the Miranda rule. After spending months defending the superiority of our civilian justice system the Obama administration thus unilaterally offered to surrender a vital civil liberties protection to the forces of moronic misrule at the very moment it was engaged in moving the Supreme Court decisively to the right in a masterstroke of pragmatic triangulation. The timing was ironic, because all we really know about Kagan's constitutional views is that she has consistently supported her president's assertions of executive power. During her confirmation hearings when she was nominated to be Obama's solicitor general, Kagan endorsed the view that a person merely suspected of financing terrorists should be subject to indefinite detention without trial. She also endorsed the Bushite doctrine that the president of the United States has the power to indefinitely detain suspected terrorists anywhere in the world.

The deadline to close Guantánamo has come and gone; perhaps the camp will be shut someday, but the Guantánamo effect will persist whether extrajudicial prisoners are held at that particular base, or in a supermax prison somewhere in the Midwest, or in a U.S. facility in Afghanistan. In November 2009, Attorney General Eric Holder boldly announced that Khalid Sheikh Mohammed, who allegedly planned the 9/11 attacks and was apparently waterboarded 183 times, would be tried in federal court in New York City. Unfortunately, Holder also announced that five other prisoners would be tried in military commissions, in keeping with the three-tiered justice system that Obama had announced the previous May, according to which prisoners will be tried in civilian court, tried in a military tribunal, or held indefinitely without trial, depending, it seems, upon the quality of the government's evidence against them—and, presumably, how much illegal torture they have suffered. The idea that Mohammed would be given the benefit of a fair and legal trial provoked an outcry from the Bushites that was as loud as it was hypocritical. Hundreds of suspected terrorists have been tried and convicted in civilian courts since 2001, whereas precisely three have been successfully tried by military commissions, and two of those allegedly dangerous terrorists have already served their sentences. Cowed by the onslaught, the White House seems to have retreated again, and although it will no doubt hold some trials—as in the military commission already under way, trying a young man captured and tortured when he was a child of fifteen, who has spent one-third of his life in Guantánamo—the Obama administration will probably give up on trials for most of these suspects; it is far easier politically simply to hold them indefinitely in the extrajudicial limbo of preventive detention.

President Obama has made permanent the enormous increase in military spending since 2001. His budget projections through 2017 allocate $4.8 trillion for the Defense Department, compared with $4.6 trillion spent by Bush over eight years. Given the escalation in Afghanistan, however, it is likely that Obama will spend more than $5 trillion on the military—more, in inflation-adjusted terms, than has been spent during any eight-year period since 1946. The number of U.S. troops in Iraq has been euphemistically "drawn down"—as of May 2010 there were 92,000—but all evidence suggests that we will never fully withdraw. In 2010, American military contractors were still building permanent bases all over that shattered country, and even if every single American soldier were to be withdrawn (a condition no competent observer ever expects to see), an army of unaccountable mercenaries employed by the United States is still by any substantive definition an American occupation force. In December, when Obama announced his surge in Afghanistan, the Congressional Research Service reported that the 30,000 new troops would be accompanied by up to 56,000 additional private contractors. As of May 2010, according to the official Pentagon figures, there were 112,092 private military contractors in Afghanistan and 95,461 in Iraq, with 42,782 in other U.S. Central Command locations, for a total of 250,335. The official total is very likely to be a significant undercount, of course, and it does not include the contractors employed by other agencies, such as the State Department and USAID, nor does it include those working for the CIA.

Inevitably, as the Bushite policies took hold, the administration began to shed its token reformers. Gregory Craig—the White House counsel and early Obama supporter who was most closely associated with the initial push to roll back the abuses of power—suddenly resigned under pressure in November after being blamed by the White House political operation for entangling Obama in disputes with the national security establishment. Craig had clearly lost the support of the president, who by now was basking in the praise of the *Wall Street Journal*'s editorial board for his prudent adoption of the core elements of Bush's global war on terror, even if he preferred to downplay that dubious distinction and to use less inflammatory language. Dawn Johnsen's nomination to head the disgraced Office of Legal Counsel had been held up in the Senate along with many other nominations; and when Obama finally was emboldened by his glorious victory over the forces of health-care reaction to make recess appointments in March 2010, he made only fifteen, the precise number that Bush had made by that point in his first term. Dawn Johnsen was not among them. After spending a year of her life in limbo, Johnsen got the message and withdrew her nomination.

Obama also continued Reagan's and Bush's approach to signing statements, declaring these line-item vetos, which are manifestly unfounded in law, to be "a legitimate constitutional function." Echoing the unitary-executive theorists, he declared that he would not permit Congress to "unduly interfere with my constitutional authority in the area of foreign affairs." Likewise, he considered congressional limitations on the use of funds to be examples of "legislative aggrandizement" and instructed his executive subordinates to treat these "requests as nonbinding." After being rebuked by Congress, Obama made a tactical retreat; better to hold the use of signing statements in reserve than to risk a court judgment that the practice is unconstitutional.

To our nation's enduring shame, Obama has consistently and strenuously resisted all attempts to hold the Bushite war criminals accountable. He demands that we look forward, not backward, but never explains how such a stance comports with his promise to restore the rule of law. Bush created a culture of lawlessness; Obama has cultivated one of impunity.

Unless, that is, you make the mistake of committing an infraction that *weakens* executive power, as did Thomas Drake, who worked for the National Security Agency under Bush, and who has now been indicted for leaking details of Bush's illegal wiretapping program. Pause, now, and consider this fact. Obama has refused to investigate unambiguous criminal behavior that was a matter of deliberate presidential policy. He has refused to prosecute or even investigate war crimes committed by policy makers. He has refused even to consider a truth commission to investigate abuses of power, the fraudulent pretext of the Iraq War, or the manner in which torture came to be a proud and public U.S. policy. His mantra with regard to government criminality has been consistent: *We must look forward, not backward!* Yet his Department of Justice has now indicted a public servant who, according to the government at least, risked his career and his personal freedom to expose elements of that vast criminal enterprise.

Obama declared the end of waterboarding, a form of torture that the Bush administration had long ago ceased to use, but made certain to retain the discretion to use more humane—kinder, gentler—forms of torture. He ordered the closure of the CIA's black sites, but worded the order so narrowly that it would not apply to functionally identical legal black holes run by military intelligence agencies such as the Joint Special Operations Command (JSOC), which reportedly controls the black site at Bagram Naval Air Station in Afghanistan, where illiterate sheep traders and auto parts dealers have been held for months, tortured with sleep deprivation, then released with a terse apology. Detainees who have spoken to the American press report that beatings and other forms of abuse continue to take place in the secret jail. "They said, 'Please accept our apology, and we are sorry that we kept you here for this time.' And that was it," one former prisoner told an American reporter. "They kept me for more than 10 months and gave me nothing back."

Torture continues. The wars continue. Rendition and secret imprisonment continue. Blanket surveillance of the American people continues—though much of that may well be legal now under the shameful FISA bill for which Senator Obama voted. State secrets, executive privilege, sovereign immunity, and executive usurpation continue. Transparency and accountability proved to be figments of the candidate's and the electorate's hopeful imaginations.

Through all of these outrages, even as it became fully manifest that hope and change had been transformed by the alchemy of power into continuity and cynical realpolitik, many of Obama's liberal supporters have sought to keep the faith, excusing his actions and conveniently forgetting their principled stand against the lawlessness of the Bush regime. It is difficult to avoid the conclusion that they were not truly outraged by the news from Abu Ghraib or Guantánamo or Bagram, from the dark secret torture cells in Egypt or in far-off Romania or Poland. Perhaps they were just angry that Bush had bragged about his crimes, that he had trampled on their precious humanitarian pieties, that he had offended the decorum of discreet hypocrisy. Or perhaps their opposition to Bush's crimes was merely opportunistic, and they simply wished to damage their partisan opponent. Or perhaps the administration's apologists have been seduced by the idea that wise and responsible rulers such as Barack Obama can be trusted with absolute powers. "If men were angels, no government would be necessary," Madison observed. "If angels were to govern men, neither external nor internal controls on government would be necessary." With the coming of the Archangel Obama, apparently, the great difficulty of obliging government to control itself has been overcome. How blessed are we to enjoy such angelic governance.

Meanwhile, back in Af-Pak, the legendary mercenaries of Blackwater were busy directing covert assassinations and kidnappings of suspected militants in Pakistan, where the company, which changed its name to Xe Services in an effort to lower its profile, reportedly runs top-secret black operations for JSOC, including many of the Predator drone attacks that have killed hundreds of Pakistani civilians. Such targeted killings, as they are called, have increased dramatically under Obama. In 2009, Obama ordered more drone attacks than Bush did in eight years. He ordered his first drone attack on his third day in office.

Although the administration prefers not to use the word, these killings are nothing but assassinations, which the United States pretends to abhor. Assassinations, furthermore, are banned under an executive order signed by Gerald Ford in 1976, though Obama could lift that ban with the stroke of his executive pen, and perhaps he secretly has lifted it. Targeted killings carried out by flying robots are not different, in terms of international law, from murders carried out by a squad of assassins. Philip Alston, the United Nations special rapporteur on extrajudicial, summary, or arbitrary executions, warned the Obama administration in October 2009 that its assassination program was probably illegal under international law and that the administration's refusal to justify the program was untenable. No doubt there exist secret OLC memos splitting the metaphysical hairs of executive doctrine to justify these extrajudicial killings, and perhaps someday we will see them (the ACLU has filed a suit seeking the legal rationale). For now, we have a speech, given in March 2010, by a lawyer at the State Department, Harold Koh, in which he assured his audience that the program conforms with "all applicable laws, including the laws of war." As during the Bush era, we are asked to give the president and his war policies our unconditional trust. John Bellinger, a lawyer for the National Security Council under George W. Bush, praised the speech: "I did not see him say anything that was different from the previous administration's legal thinking." The Pakistani government has reportedly acquiesced in the killings and even gives its own targets to the Americans. A study of the drone attacks by the New American Foundation concluded that the civilian casualty rate of the attacks was about 32 percent, feeding Pakistanis' hatred of both the United States and its own weak central government.

In January, the Obama administration leaked word to the press that an American citizen named Anwar al-Awlaki had been targeted by the government for extrajudicial assassination. It was explained—by unnamed sources, naturally— that this man is a dangerous terrorist who is plotting to kill Americans. Allegedly he is hiding in Yemen. Representative

Jane Harmon, who chairs the Homeland Security Subcommittee on Intelligence, went on the record to say that Awlaki is "probably the person, the terrorist, who would be terrorist No. 1 in terms of threat against us." A bigger threat than Osama bin Laden? How could this be? What crimes has the man committed? We are told that he provides inspiration to terrorists; that he was in contact with Umar Farouk Abdulmutallab, the hapless underwear bomber; that his writings and Internet sermons inspired Faisal Shahzad, the man accused of trying to bomb Times Square; and that he has been linked to Nidal Malik Hasan, the army psychologist charged with killing thirteen people at Fort Hood. Our leading newspapers have run long stories detailing the enormity of this preacher's hatred for the United States, which he believes has declared war on Islam; but these newspapers betray few hints that the Obama administration might itself be committing a war crime by targeting him for assassination. Unnamed intelligence officials claim that Awlaki has assumed an "operational role" in Al Qaeda on the Arabian Peninsula; but anyone familiar with the long list of the CIA's blunders—the record of innocent men kidnapped, rendered, and tortured only to be set free with an apology or left to rot in Guantánamo—can only respond with skepticism to such claims. Perhaps Awlaki is worse than Osama bin Laden, but isn't that what trials are for? Because Awlaki is an American citizen, who was born in New Mexico, we have been assured that the approval for the assassination order had to come from the National Security Council.

The radicalism of the executive prerogative in this case

is breathtaking, yet such is the state of American justice. According to our laws, tapping an American's telephone line requires a court order, but our chief magistrate claims the power to execute summarily a citizen who is not personally engaged in violent activity or combat. Apparently, this is what Obama means by pragmatism: that laws may be suspended at will in the name of convenience. We shall simply murder our ideological adversaries, and like Bush we will brag about it in the press, blithely assuming that such crimes will silence the chorus of enemies. What all-important tactical aim will the extrajudicial murder of this American citizen achieve? His sermons are already widely available; his incitements would live on after him, endowed with a made-in-America aura of martyrdom. If anything, Awlaki's assassination would constitute a proof of his argument.

Under Barack Obama, in the calmest, most reasonable tones of voice, an American citizen has been accused, tried, convicted, and sentenced to death in absentia by the sole and absolute authority of the duly elected monarch of the United States. It is as if Thomas Jefferson, after defeating the Federalists in 1800, had taken office and immediately applied the hated provisions of the Sedition Act to his political enemies. As James Madison wrote in *The Federalist*, "The accumulation of all powers legislative, executive and judiciary, in the same hands, whether of one, a few or many, and whether hereditary, self-appointed or elective, may justly be pronounced the very definition of tyranny." The mere existence of such arbitrary power is absolutely destructive of liberty.

CHAPTER NINE

————

SPEAK, MONEY

Americans have long preferred to view their politics in terms of recurrent waves of liberalism and conservatism. "During periods of inaction," wrote Arthur M. Schlesinger Jr., "unsolved social problems pile up till the demand for reform becomes overwhelming. Then a liberal government comes to power, the dam breaks and a flood of change sweeps away a great deal in a short time. After fifteen or twenty years the liberal impulse is exhausted, the day of 'consolidation' and inaction arrives, and conservatism, once again, expresses the mood of the country, but generally on the terms of the liberalism it displaces." Unfortunately, this is an exceedingly optimistic and even naive view of American history, though it does at least recognize the tendency of old terms to endure long after they have ceased to carry any political weight. The conservative-liberal opposition conceals more than it reveals, and it assumes that history marches in one direction. Obama's presidency, which ought to have been a Jeffersonian return to principle after the reign of the Bushite witches, may stand as its decisive rebuttal. Instead of returning us to the constitutional norm, Obama has squandered his historic opportunity and institutionalized the witchcraft, coming up with better and smarter spells, but pursuing the same pernicious ends.

The central terms of our politics—liberal, conservative, democratic, and republican—play a game of partisan musical chairs, with doctrines concerning such supposedly essential matters as states' rights and executive power switching places every few decades and assuming ever-finer gradations of meaning, the terms attaching themselves to one party or another, depending on the fashion of the times. As was noted already during the debate over the Constitution, even the term "federalist" was deeply equivocal, and if the party of Adams and Hamilton had not taken up that label, it might with more justice have been employed by the party of Madison, who was far more concerned than his opponents to respect the balance of powers envisioned by the Constitution. Despite our terminal semantic confusions, however, it is possible to discern a clear pattern of philosophical polarity running through American history, a line of conflict that transcends the traditional division of our history into three distinct party systems, and those systems into two distinct parties: Madisonian republicanism versus Hamiltonian autocracy. Over time both dominant parties have gradually acquired a Hamiltonian core, even as they both employed a superficial republican rhetoric. True republicans have always been a minority among us, haunting the margins of the dominant parties, occasionally mounting sorties on Washington, only to fail or in victory fall victim to corruption. No wonder that busy citizens, distracted by the increasingly difficult task of making a living in a society that insists on destroying its most valuable industries, began to lose the thread. Finally, the mass media succeeded in scattering to the far reaches of the spectrum and the dusty paranoid culs-de-sac of cyberspace whatever historical consciousness had remained among the citizenry. Politics descended into a realm of pure fiction and thirty-second storytelling. Today we are treated to a battle of postmodernist narratives rather than policies, and candidates for our attention prance across our television screens to be praised and censored by media personalities whose primary job qualification and highly marketable skill consists of an ability to keep talking in front of a camera no matter what happens.

And yet politics continues to have vital—in some cases mortal—consequences for most people, even as our alleged representatives permit themselves to be corrupted by wealth and patronage and to busy themselves above all in the disbursal of legislative goodies for contributors and the stockpiling of moneys for advertisements to manipulate the public into casting votes, while our interchangeable unitary executives busy themselves with everlasting glory both at home and abroad. What we are left with today, with the ascendency of the Archangel Obama, is the Triumph of the Hamiltonian

Will. Our public life is dominated by two Federalist parties, both of which to varying degrees pay lip service to the republican tradition. We have out-Hamiltoned Hamilton, and the corruption that Madison and Jefferson feared is so complete that most of us have lost the capacity to see it clearly. We know something is wrong—we feel it even if we lack the information to give our feelings rational content—but our political vocabulary is inadequate to the task of opposition. The discourse of conservatism and liberalism is utterly inadequate given the nature of our political affliction. Republican theory, however, offers us resources that have not been fully exploited.

The public sphere is filled with a welter of rival languages, vocabularies, discourses, idioms of legitimation. None of them today enjoys a monopoly. We have religious idioms, theologico-political idioms, those that are called conservative, and those labeled liberal. Most citizens and even most partisans, however, are not capable of rigorously distinguishing one from another. These vocabularies come into and go out of vogue and are used in different contexts depending on particular objectives. Very often those who engage in political debate rely on utterly different sets of assumptions or are committed to irreconcilable principles, with the result that whoever screams loudest is deemed the winner, especially in the all-important news cycle. By far the most common rhetoric employed by contemporary political antagonists is that of freedom, though here, too, there are competing concepts, many of which are hopelessly muddled. Several years ago, for example, I was given a T-shirt, purchased at the military gift shop of Camp X-Ray at Guantánamo Naval Base, that bore the slogan "THERE'S NOWHERE TO HIDE FROM FREEDOM." What is this freedom that seeks out enemies, tortures them, and imprisons them in tiny cells without trial? Such freedom, from which no terrorist or shifty Muslim can hide, clearly signifies the relentless and irresistible military might of the American empire. Perhaps this is the freedom for which Ronald Reagan's Nicaraguan and Afghan freedom fighters were fighting in the 1980s; it is very far from the idea of liberty enshrined in the Declaration of Independence.

Domestically, the word "freedom" usually conveys a different meaning. In the language of market fundamentalism, the dominant idiom of establishment economics and Wall Street corporatism, freedom is simply choice—the choice to buy one pair of sneakers or another; the choice to watch a movie starring Keanu Reeves doing computer-enhanced backflips or a TV show depicting American secret agents torturing villains to stop a nuclear bomb from destroying Los Angeles. More high-flown and philosophical discussions of freedom emphasize the absence of constraint—the absence of limits, in other words—and this is in fact the conventional concept of freedom in the liberal philosophical tradition. It is the freedom of Thomas Hobbes, whose definition is worth quoting: "By liberty, is understood, according to the proper signification of the word, the absence of external impediments: which impediments, may oft take away part of a man's power to do what he would; but cannot hinder him from using the power left him, according as his judgment, and reason shall dictate to him." Whether defined in positive terms of choice or in terms of the absence of limit, impediment, or constraint, this notion of freedom has come in our day to be seen in largely economic terms; freedom of choice is but a freedom to shop, to follow one's volitions and whims, constrained only by law, where freedom ends. So understood, freedom is negative, and it is distinguished, as in Isaiah Berlin's classic account, from positive freedom: freedom as agency, autonomy; freedom as civic virtue, political participation, ruling and being ruled—all of which Berlin associates with troubling doctrines such as Marxism and premodern republicanism. Positive freedom, for many philosophical liberals, is thought to be slightly scary, vaguely coercive, perhaps totalitarian. Freedom as the absence of limit also naturally comports with the modern liberal state's ideology of growth and expansion; economies must continually grow, and so too must consumers' choice.

The republican tradition, which to be sure is part of the broader liberal tradition, conveys a rival understanding of liberty; and it is republican liberty, taken together with its critique of civil corruption, that is most pertinent to our current political predicament. Despite the varied and often incompatible uses of the word "freedom" that we encounter in the American public sphere—in the angry rantings of Tea Partiers no less than in the chants of striking workers on the picket line—one can often detect lurking beneath the surface, as an unexamined premise, a rhetoric of liberty according to which domination or dependency is the great evil to be avoided.

Liberty, for republicans, is an irreducibly political concept. It exists not in the absence of restraint but in the absence of an arbitrary or dominating will. If you are vulnerable to the arbitrary will of an individual or group that somehow contrives to take power over you and to enforce its will upon you, then you are not at liberty. Such a state is, in republican terms, unfreedom, servitude, slavery. Nothing is more obnoxious than the arbitrary will of a master—whether that master is a king, a policeman, or an agent of Homeland Security who at his whim may dispose of my life or my property. In fact, the Latin *obnoxius* originally signified precisely the predicament of living in subservience and later came to describe, in English republican discourse, the objectionable conduct of slavish and cringing dependents. The vagaries of bureaucratic caprice, in which a functionary has arbitrary and willful discretion over some aspect of my life, the brutal father who can beat his wife or children without fear of sanction or consequence, or the employer who adheres to the oxymoronic right-to-work doctrine of at-will employment and thus has the power to dispose of an employee's livelihood on a whim—all of these figures exemplify the tyrannical and arbitrary will that republican theory has always deplored. Individuals who are subject to such domination live in the shadow of violence, whether physical, emotional, or economic. Such servitude leads to flattery, kowtowing sycophancy, and other degrading and contemptible behavior.

A classic illustration of the difference between the two understandings of freedom is that of the slave whose benevolent master permits him to do whatever he wishes. Such a slave is free from constraint and yet is nevertheless a slave;

the master may change his mind, die, or sell the slave. A slave lives under the constant threat of domination, and even if he lives his whole life without ever having to submit to unreasonable or unjust demands, there is no proper sense in which he is free. Advocates of the republican idea of freedom point out that freedom as noninterference may result because powerful individuals happen to show you favor, or because you cleverly manage to avoid their attention, or because you are particularly skilled in the arts of flattery and ingratiation. Republicans are likely to despise the choices afforded by such freedom.

Freedom as nondomination is thus more robust, both conceptually and politically, than the conventional idea of freedom of choice, because it necessarily entails noninterference and, where it is secure, implies positive security over one's independence. If no one can dominate you, no one can impose arbitrary limits on your activities. To be at liberty is thus to be empowered, to possess the control that an active and flourishing human being enjoys over his or her own destiny. As Trenchard and Gordon put it in *Cato's Letters*: "Liberty is, to live upon one's own Terms; slavery is, to live at the mere mercy of another; and a life of slavery is, to those who can bear it, a continual state of uncertainty and wretchedness, often an apprehension of violence, often the lingering dread of a violent death." Freedom of choice, moreover, may exist in any governmental system, whereas republican freedom presupposes some mechanism of popular government through which law is legitimized. The highest form of freedom arises from a regime in which the citizen participates in government—in the classic formulation, by ruling and being ruled.

Good law creates liberty, and rule of law is a necessary condition of liberty. Law can also be unjust, coercive, and destructive of freedom if it becomes the instrument of an arbitrary will, whether of an individual or a group. Obama's health-care legislation fails the test of liberty in republican terms because it serves the interests of insurers and other corrupt interests who demanded the insurance mandate and cut a deal to kill a health plan that would not have favored private profit over public health. Consequently, every American will soon be compelled, directly or indirectly, to purchase a product that will enrich private companies. It is, in effect, not only a tax but a new and perverse form of tax farming that guarantees profits for private firms by compelling the purchase of a product (an insurance policy), which by no means guarantees access to the public good (medical care) that the law is allegedly designed to achieve. Nor does it do anything to control the exponentially growing costs of our irrational health system, another of the law's purported goals. The insurance mandate is arbitrary because it was advanced as an act of will on the part of certain business groups precisely in order to further their private interests and profitability.

Medical care could have been made available in a variety of different ways that would not have required individuals to support the continued profitability of parasites, which add no value whatsoever to the transactions between doctors and patients. If Congress decided to levy a direct tax on all citizens to fund a public health plan, that would not be an arbitrary levy—even if I disagreed with the aims of the tax or wished I didn't have to pay it. The mandate, furthermore, is factional in the worst sense, because it serves primarily to enrich a particular group: health-care profiteers who are unnecessary for the achievement of the social interest of providing access to medical care. A basic premise of the republican form of government is our agreement to submit to law that we arrive at publicly, through a legitimate deliberative process. The illegitimate bargains on which ObamaCare is premised manifestly fail to meet this standard.

Mere freedom of choice, if that is the principle of our politics, gives us no critical purchase, no ammunition with which to fight the imposition of arbitrary will. If my government imposes upon me an unjust law that still leaves me with a menu of choices, on what grounds may I contest it? Am I not subject to the laws of the land? Am I not given choices? Isn't freedom of choice my highest civic value? Freedom of choice need not be despised, of course, but choice and the pleasures of shopping for whatever entices our animal spirits falls more properly within the domain of happiness and its pursuit. If, on the contrary, our highest civic value is freedom as nondomination, the liberty that arises when I am my own master—in other words, the liberty in the name of which our revolutionary generation declared its independence—then we possess a critical concept with which to do battle against the forces that seek to oppress us. Republican rhetoric is preeminently a rhetoric of contestation, and liberty must be continually asserted and defended at all times.

Any child possesses a sense of justice, and nothing of-

fends justice more than arbitrary rule—decisions that depend
on the corrupt whim or self-interested judgment of a person
in authority rather than on a general rule that applies to all
without exception and aims only at the largest possible public
interest. Americans may disagree about many things, but no
one wishes to live in servitude. About that, at least, most of
us can agree. When it comes to law and civil regulation, the
power of money in politics means that those who can pay
for access to government receive special treatment, loopholes,
carve-outs, earmarks, and other unjust grants of funds and
privilege. Those who govern us cease to be representatives
and become rulers; severed from their intended dependency
on the people, they align themselves with those on whom
they do depend and pursue their own private interests, which
all too often harmonize with the exercise of military power
and the glory they derive therefrom. Witness the long emergency that has afflicted us since September 11, 2001, and the
sustained attack on our civil liberties and our constitutional
protections by government prerogative. How could our historical commitment to liberal government be overturned by
an attack, horrific as it was, that imposed a few thousand ca-
sualties? Perhaps it was because we had already drifted far
away from our republican and democratic roots. After every
new terrorist incident our leaders compete to see who can de-
vise more extreme and tyrannical responses, with Joe Lieberman invariably capturing the laurels. After the failed attack
on Times Square, Lieberman and the freshman senator Scott
Brown proposed legislation that would strip citizenship from
anyone merely *suspected* of involvement with terrorism.

The fundamental political questions of republicanism are as operative today as they were in 1689, 1776, or 1789. Do our institutions foster the development of a civic personality or one that is merely private and self-absorbed? Do they encourage autonomy and agency or dependence? Are we subject to arbitrary force? Liberal institutions such as Social Security, Medicare, and the modern regulatory apparatus should be evaluated in those terms. At their best, these social programs should be seen as institutions that are productive of personal autonomy and liberty because they provide a modest foundation of material security, a guarantee that we will not starve, go without shelter, perish from avoidable illness, or be exploited by monopolies. They are meant to free us from the arbitrary sway of employers and large companies, and from the vagaries of an irrational marketplace—to give dignity to the lives of working people. These benign institutions, however, have been under attack from the very moment they were created; corporate ideologues despise them precisely because they weaken the dependency of citizens on large employers. And like all human creations, they are are subject to decay and corruption, and if well constituted must incorporate checks and balances to ensure that they do not themselves become the instrument of arbitrary administrative and bureaucratic power. Like all government institutions, they may be abused and thus require an occasional return to first principles.

In the latest round of hand-wringing over the federal budget deficit, a debt generated above all by wars, financial bailouts, tax cuts for the rich, and a recession caused by the bursting of the housing bubble, the renewed focus on the

few public institutions that are specifically designed to protect the dignity of the least powerful members of our society
has nothing to do with protecting liberty. As Ben Bernanke,
in moment of candor, told a congressional committee, Social
Security is simply where the money is. Mendacious politicians
who would prefer not to challenge the interests of the most
powerful elements of our society naturally find themselves
coveting funds devoted to the security and well-being of wid-
ows and orphans. Obama, for his part, has been cagey and
vague about Social Security and other so-called entitlements,
but his repeated insistence that "everything is on the table"
when it comes to reducing the federal budget deficit should
give us pause. If everything were truly on the table, of course,
we might have a vigorous national debate about whether a
military budget that is rapidly approaching $1 trillion a year
is truly necessary, or whether our Asiatic wars truly serve the
national interest. Perhaps new fees on financial transactions—
a simple measure that would also serve to curb the licentious-
ness of runaway financial schemes and destructive trading
programs—should be considered, or more aggressive taxation of corporations, which enjoy constitutional protection
for their political spending but currently avoid most income
taxes. Two-thirds of the 1.3 million corporations active in the
United States in 2008 paid zero income tax between 1998 and
2005; in 2009 General Electric, which reported $10.3 bil-
lion in pretax income, paid no federal taxes. Instead, when
Obama's bipartisan commission on debt reduction, which was
duly stacked with known advocates of cutting social services,
announces its recommendations in December 2010, safely

after the midterm elections, we can expect to hear the tired canting of millionaires about the necessity for middle- and lower-income Americans to make hard choices about the social programs that serve their interests.

KARL MARX WAS NOT WRONG when he wrote that "the history of all hitherto existing society is the history of class struggles." But his concept of class was too speculative, and his romanticism led him and his disciples to identify a particular class as the carrier of world history. With no little historical irony he attempted to burden the working classes with the hard labor of smashing through the iron cage of history. For all his dialectical brilliance, it turned out that the cage was far less brittle than he had anticipated. Other thinkers, among them the founding legislators of the American system of government, also saw the history of all hitherto existing societies in terms of class, but their view of class was neither so rigid nor so optimistic. Class, for the republicans whose thought informs our system of government, was not a cause or an underlying trans-historical substance but an effect, an effect of interest. Conflicts of such interests are the essence of politics, and their energy, within the peaceful confines of a well-designed and well-regulated constitution, produces the health of the state, a tense equilibrium in which varied interests hold one another at bay and thereby fashion a mode of accommodation, a modus vivendi, that must be continuously renegotiated.

Interest breeds faction, and faction breeds party. If a party system denies interest a proper outlet, the system will over time lose its stability and degenerate into mere rotation of personnel, an endless cycling of corrupt officers attended by rising frustration and by clamors among the populace. Contrary to our national mythology, it has been the active combinations and pecuniary dispensations of business coalitions that have largely driven our politics since the eighteenth century. At various times those moneyed interests have made concessions to the general interests of the public, and for a brief interlude, lasting a few decades in the middle of the twentieth century, the public interest came close to achieving parity with the costly pageantry and venal spirit of the Hamiltonian system. No longer. For the last thirty years, the public has suffered a dramatic reversal at the hands of the moneyed interests as the latter have vied with one another for control of the state, though their common agenda is plain enough to see from a comparison of the luxury goods on display along Madison Avenue with the shuttered small businesses that line the Main Streets of the American heartland.

Republican political thought is not hostile to wealth or property, but it assumes a balance of property, a moderate distribution of wealth. The balance of wealth in the United States, after that brief period of temperance following World War II, has been lost. Make no mistake—this was by no means a golden age; it was a time of strife, contestation, and the expansion of an international military and commercial empire. I point merely to the relative moderation of its material basis, which might have been the foundation for a renaissance in self-government. The social revolutions of that period transformed our society, but they did not succeed in transforming our government, which succumbed to the swelling cancer that had long afflicted it. It is often claimed that the gap between rich and poor began to widen in the late 1970s, as if to absolve Ronald Reagan for what his followers no doubt count as his primary accomplishment; but the total share of income of the wealthiest 10 percent of American families was well within the postwar norm until 1982—it was rising in the late 1970s but under Carter had not even reached Johnsonian levels. After Ronald Reagan came into office the trend line became almost vertical as federal economic policies encouraged an unprecedented transfer of national wealth to the rich. Aside from occasional recessionary setbacks, the slope continued to rise over the next three decades. Under Bill Clinton, the change was even more dramatic than it was under Reagan: between 1994 and 2000, the top 10 percent increased its share of the national income from 40.8 percent to 47.6 percent. By 2007, the wealthiest 10 percent, families earning more than $109,630, was capturing 50 percent of the national income.

Even among the rich the disparities are significant: the superrich top 1 percent of Americans earned far more than those in the next nine percentiles. In 1980 the superrich received 10 percent of the national income; by 2007 the superrich had increased their share to 23.5 percent; and the next 4 percent on the income scale managed to increase its share only from 13.2 percent to 15.2 percent—not much of a gain. The next 5 percent down, the 90–95th percentile, saw its share of the national wealth *decrease* from 11.5 percent to 11.1 percent. In fact, the bottom 99 percent of American earners saw nowhere near the rise in average real income that the top 1 percent did. The average increase—in terms of real income, not the percentage share of total national income— for the bottom 99 percent of American families between 1973 and 2006 was a mere 8.5 percent, whereas the richest 1 percent of families saw a *190 percent rise* in real income. As with their increasing slice of the national economic pie, the rise in personal income really accelerated after Reagan's economic policies went into effect. In 1980, the average earned income of the superrich, the top 1 percent, was $320,861; in 2007 that had risen to $952,388. By comparison, the average income of the bottom 99 percent was $36,396 in 1980, and by 2007 it had risen all the way to $42,986.

That last set of comparisons is particularly revealing, because it shows just how small a portion of the population has experienced most of the income gains over the last forty years. Moreover, the pattern holds across parties. A comparison of the income gains of the superrich under Bill Clinton and under George W. Bush is startling. In 1993, under Clinton, the average family in the top percentile was earning $531,842; by 2000 that figure was $843,599—a 59 percent increase. Under Bush the income of the superrich had risen only to $952,388—a mere 13 percent gain. Purely in terms of earned income, the Bush years were very good for the superrich, but the Clinton years were even better. In terms of rising inequality, however, the Bush years were far worse. During the Clinton expansion, the superrich 1 percent captured

45 percent of the national income growth, whereas under the Bush expansion the superrich captured 65 percent.

Such distortions of the nation's balance of wealth did not come about by accident, by the actions of impersonal forces such as Obama's relentless pools and advances. They were the result of a raft of policy decisions—about industry and trade, taxation and military spending by flesh-and-blood humans, sitting in concrete-and-steel buildings—that were bought and paid for by the less than *1 percent of Americans* who participate in our oligarchy by contributing at least $200 to political campaigns. Not only do gross inequalities in wealth distort the political economy, creating a perverse feedback loop in which the interests of the wealthy and the centers of power in government recede ever farther from those of the general public; such inequality also introduces significant distortions into the political psychology of voters. Some of the best recent empirical work in political science has shown that most Americans *attempt* to vote in accordance with their economic interests, rather than with the dictates of ephemeral antagonisms over God, gays, or guns. Most lower-income Americans, even poor whites in red states, vote for Democrats because they believe, rightly, that they will fare better under the rule of this degenerate party. On the other hand, most upper-income Americans, even rich whites in blue states, vote for Republicans because they believe, wrongly, that they will fare better under *that* degenerate party. As it happens, a recent analysis of relative income growth under Democratic and Republican administrations concluded that almost all Americans are better off economically under Democrats.

Unfortunately, for the vast majority of Americans economic improvement has been so marginal that it is easily overshadowed by cynical manipulations of the political business cycle, i.e., the timing of economic expansions with election years (Republicans are better at this, historically), and by the strange fact that lower-income voters are more sensitive, in terms of voting behavior, to income growth among the wealthy than they are to their own economic well-being. Meanwhile, since the early 1980s, the Democratic Party has largely abandoned its commitment to policies that serve the material interests of most Americans. Add to these complexities the proven power of campaign spending to influence election outcomes (Larry Bartels has calculated that each additional dollar spent per voter by a candidate increases the probability of a given undecided voter's support by almost 4 percentage points), and it is easy to see that the average American has no hope of safeguarding his or her interests, whether they pertain to life, liberty, or happiness. The costs our society imposes on participation are simply too high. Consequently, we are very far from the classical republican ideal of ruling and being ruled, of exercising political agency and participating in the life of our commonwealth—indeed, we are incapable of even pursuing narrow self-interest very effectively—and are instead rendered impotent, obsequious, the unresisting tools of interests we scarcely comprehend.

Mere campaign-finance reform is not enough. Given the scale of the present corruption, a more radical remedy is clearly needed. In January 2010, in *Citizens United v. Federal Election Commission*, the United States Supreme Court held that restrictions on independent corporate expenditures in political campaigns (as opposed to direct political contributions) are unconstitutional restrictions on the freedom of speech. Much of the judicial literature on the subject, including Justice Anthony Kennedy's majority opinion in *Citizens United*, simply substitutes the words "speech" and "speak" for the words "spend" and "buy." Corporations, according to the court's majority faction, are speakers, persons who have constitutional rights. When they spend, they speak. Kennedy admits that favoritism and influence can result from campaign spending, but he asserts that far from being objectionable or avoidable, favoritism and influence are the essence of representative politics, that it is right and natural for a representative to favor certain "voters and contributors." Indeed, he continues, "it is well understood that a substantial and legitimate reason, if not the only reason, to cast a vote for, or to make a contribution to, one candidate over another is that the candidate will respond by producing those political outcomes the supporter favors. Democracy is premised on responsiveness." With admirable frankness if less than impeccable logic, Kennedy equates not only the act of spending money with speech but also the act of making a campaign contribution with voting. The idea of corruption resulting from the quid pro quo of contribution for legislation troubles him not at all. "The appearance of influence or access, furthermore," he repeats, as if a lie may be converted into truth by mere reiteration, "will not cause the electorate to lose faith in our democracy."

If there were any doubts about what sort of government we live under, Kennedy's opinion should lay them to rest.

We can still say we live in a commercial republic, yes, but only in the sense that our most sovereign activity has been transmuted by the alchemy of our shadow constitution into a commercial exchange: instead of ruling and being ruled we buy and are bought, and thereby express our commercial virtue. Indeed, civic virtue has now completed its centuries-long metamorphosis from the republican ideal of the free citizen-ruler to the degraded economic norm of the consumer buying on credit; virtue for us is no more than a spotless credit rating. Thus the terror of a credit crisis; it strikes at the very foundation of public personality. The more abstract and financialized our commercial expressions are, the more virtuous they become; therefore corporations, fictional beings of pure commerce, predicated on our collective fantasies, are now the highest expression of political art. Corporations are evolving under judicial legislation into the perfect, immortal citizen-rulers of our capitalist democracy, a virtual republic in which all political speech is advertising and all real citizens are commercial fictions.

It is a curious metaphysical doctrine, is it not? Corporations are artificial beings, theoretically immortal, which come into existence by means of state charters and reproduce like amoebas by splitting into subsidiaries; midwifed by lawyers, they combine in bizarre mating rituals called mergers; they are owned, like slaves, by shareholders who buy and sell their chattel daily; and they possess constitutional rights. Oddly, however, our corporate citizens are denied the right to vote. By what logic can a corporation be granted personhood and the constitutional right to speak money but yet be denied the constitutional right to vote? How can our system permit these corporate persons to be enslaved through ownership? Does not the force of all logic and morality require us either to deny the personhood of corporations, with its attendant paradoxes, or to grant them the right to vote and to free them from their status as slaves? And if we insist on maintaining their status as persons, at least let us give ourselves the power, if they commit serious crimes against property, to put corporations to death.

Given the weird First Amendment metaphysics to which a majority of our Supreme Court justices subscribe, it is obvious that campaign-finance reform is a dead letter, notwithstanding Obama's pious noises following the verdict in *Citizens United*. It seems only a matter of time and litigation before all limits to political expenditures are erased in the name of free speech; the radical doctrines of the Roberts Court admit no foreseeable limit. The Republican Party and its ideological lawyers in the Federalist Society thus may yet have reason to regret their determined advocacy on behalf of the heresy that money equals speech. Obama outspent McCain two-to-one during the last election, and there is no reason to believe that all or even most corporate spending will be channeled to the party of Abraham Lincoln and Sarah Palin. On the contrary, Democrats are likely to benefit as much as or more than the Republicans, even after Kennedy, Scalia, et al. finally get their chance to liberate flesh-and-blood persons, especially that wise and judicious 1 percent who wish to make their money speak, from the fetters of financial censorship and disenfranchisement.

Surely, however, the American people have not become so servile that they will forever submit to the rule of 1 percent. Surely we are capable of recognizing that the regime which has arisen from a perverse tradition of constitutional interpretation holding that money must be equated with political speech, and that corporations must enjoy all the inalienable rights (but none of the sovereign duties) of personhood, is a usurpation of popular government. Our Constitution unquestionably recognizes the right of a people to alter its mode of government; we have done so twenty-seven times. We may do so again. We may throw off these bonds and provide new guards for our future security.

CHAPTER TEN

INVENTIONS OF PRUDENCE

Constitutional devices that might begin to cure the pe- cuniary cancers that have corrupted our political in- stitutions are not beyond the imagination. A constitutional amendment stripping corporations of the rights of person- hood would be a promising start; one might continue with an amendment designed to eliminate or minimize as far as pos- sible the use of private moneys in political campaigns. Such amendments have already been drafted; the beginnings of a movement already exist, and legislation has been introduced. I refer not to Chuck Schumer's lamentable "Disclose Act," which the senior senator from Wall Street erroneously sug- gests would counter *Citizens United* by merely strengthening disclosure requirements; we already know quite enough about

Schumer's corporate backers. Lawrence Lessig's Change Congress movement is more promising: it has inspired committed liberal political funders to withhold their support for any politician who opposes free and fair elections in the United States; it also supports the Fair Elections Now Act, a modest beginning that would create a public funding option for all federal candidates. More radically, the group has sponsored an initiative for a constitutional convention.

It should not be overly difficult to design and implement a set of statutes and a regulatory regimen that would radically curtail the ability of moneyed interests to purchase their agendas via legislation. Other countries strictly limit the duration of campaigns and the manner and venues of political expenditures. Since the public owns the broadcast spectrum, Congress could outlaw political advertising and create a variety of public channels for the expression of political speech by candidates, with suitable eligibility requirements designed to remove biases based on wealth. Or campaigns could be limited in time to a few months or even weeks, during which periods advertising could be banned but prior to which various forms of commercial speech might be financed by interest groups and corporations for the express purpose of assassinating the character of political opponents or demonizing their opinions. All kinds of political mechanisms are possible, and not only with regard to campaigns. Private lobbying might be eliminated as well, forcing all communication pertaining to legislation into public forums devised to liberate our representatives and their staffs from the burden of accommodating all those lobbyists in their schedules, thus freeing our lawmakers to master the intricacies of modern regulation. And consider all the time that could be saved by members of Congress who were no longer obliged to spend their days on the telephone begging for handouts. Lawmakers would be decent human beings again, unshackled from a servile dependency on the arbitrary willfulness of political patrons. Let us restore dignity to the profession of politics!

Nor must we necessarily limit ourselves to removing the most obvious tool of corrupt influence, the campaign contribution. Even in an ideal system of public campaign financing, in which all political speech has been equalized by law, in which political advertising is banned and persuasion stripped of its commercial aspect—even then, the businessman and the millionaire (not to mention the billionaire) would stand taller than the common citizen. In a system purged of private election money, corporations would have renewed incentives to enter the publishing business, to fund newspapers, magazines, or whatever the Internet analogue of those old forms comes to be. Wealthy citizens would still have a large advantage, by virtue of their background, education, and leisure, and would certainly continue to dominate the political class. In fact, the wealthy are likely to dominate any political regime that chooses its magistrates and officials solely by means of election.

Banishing the overt power of money from our elections would not end the strife and tumult of politics. If anything, it would increase the uproar and sharpen our divisions. Conflict in politics is not a metaphor, and as with any fight, the audience is likely to get involved; perhaps lowering the barriers to entry would be sufficient to reinvigorate the public. Even so, the natural advantage of the rich remains a problem, and not everyone agrees that they deserve to rule. Past republics, in antiquity and in the Renaissance, were particularly concerned to contain the power of the rich and prevent them from capturing the institutions of government. Constitutional devices to prevent the rule of the rich have included wealth ceilings and other confiscations that certainly would not be in keeping with American tradition, but one could place an upper limit on the net worth of elected representatives; the House could have such a limit—or, even better, the Senate, which is at present a millionaires' club. We could create tribunes of the people, permanent federal public advocates who would jealously guard the rights of the many against the depredations of the few. Quotas could also be used, or systems of lot that would inject a randomizing element into the political selection process. A slate of prospective candidates could draw lots to see who would be permitted to stand for election. Variations on all of these devices have been used by republics in the past; all would be preferable to the current system, which resembles a lottery that is decisively if imperfectly rigged in favor of those who already have millions in the bank.

Some of these legal devices are radical; others are modest. All of them are possible. What is lacking, of course, is *political will*. The moneyed interests on whom our lawmakers depend have plenty of political will, which they express in unambiguous monetary terms. Make no mistake: it is perfectly legitimate for the rich to pursue their own interests; what is not legitimate is the current exclusion of all other interests from the reason of state. Is it possible that the majority of Americans whose interests emphatically are not being served have no political will? As Madison asked long ago: Are we utterly without civic virtue? If so, then we are truly wretched. "To suppose that any form of government will secure liberty or happiness without any virtue in the people is a chimerical idea."

Although we have always benefited from the activities of public-spirited individuals, including men and women of great wealth who recognize that greed as a principle of public conduct often leads to perverse outcomes, the United States Constitution was emphatically not founded on the assumption that either citizens or magistrates could be trusted to act selflessly. If my argument can be taken as a call to republican virtue, that is so only within the modern realist framework devised in 1787 by Madison and his colleagues, according to whom government is a response to humanity's inherent wickedness. Men are not angels, Obama notwithstanding. A properly American call to republican virtue is not a utopian exhortation that our citizens cast aside their private and selfish interests and embark on a course of austere political action, with their eyes fixed on some transcendent public good apart from their own. No, what is required is that Americans take a stand *on behalf of their selfish material interests* and against those of the monopolies and transnational corporations that have captured our institutions of government. The character of our popular corruption is that the people are insufficiently selfish. Republican virtue in the American context requires the constant and vigilant assertion of the multiplicity of interests that compose our citizenry.

Our civil crisis is founded on the seeming paradox that most Americans have become slothfully selfless, too absorbed by fleeting pleasures and distractions to fight for their narrow material interests; the many have been convinced that their interests are identical with those of the few, an equation that is manifestly false. If a majority of Americans simply acted out of self-interest they would contain the rich and enact vigorous Madisonian laws that, operating silently, would reduce the power and wealth of the 1 percent who control the destiny of our corporate oligarchy. What we require, therefore, is precisely what our congressional barons and corporate overlords fear most: class warfare, though of a peaceful and democratic variety. We require a large and clamorous public movement led by a disciplined and ruthless faction willing to deny all support to politicians who refuse to conform to the anticorruption platform. Is such a movement possible? In a nation that enacted the prohibition of alcohol by constitutional amendment, anything is possible.

All government, no matter how despotic, depends ultimately on public opinion; the challenge that faces a movement of fundamental reform is that public opinion is often a mere artifact of political struggle, and our chief organs of politics today are thoroughly cancer-ridden. The only hope for citizens who are opposed to the corporate interests that dominate both parties is to fashion a movement of opinion designed to destabilize the oppositions that divide the citizenry into mindless supporters of whatever schemes the party bosses pursue. Many liberals who deplore Obama's insipid pragmatism and stand-pat conservatism nevertheless feel compelled to support him as he betrays everything they believe in. Why? Because they are afraid of right-wing marionettes like Sarah Palin and the misguided, misinformed Tea Partiers who flock to her banner. What we must recognize is that Palin and her ilk are in some ways Obama's best allies; they frighten the Democratic base into submission. Liberals who disagree with the president's policies must come to understand that the Tea Partiers are not wrong to be angry with Obama and the Democrats. Common cause should be made with self-styled conservatives and rightist libertarians like Ron Paul over the perils of arbitrary rule and the obscene combination of corporate power with the party machines. Tea Partiers have no desire to lose their Social Security or their Medicare; they may insist on gun rights but their desire for financial security is strong as well. The liberals who hate guns have to decide whether they hate firearms more than they hate arbitrary government. The principles of American republicanism ought to constitute a political lingua franca transcending the simplistic oppositions of conservative and liberal polemics. To Americans, all arbitrary power should be suspect, whether it originates in a private corporate bureaucracy, a public welfare agency, a public-private monopoly, the CIA, or the Department of Homeland Security. No doubt what I am describing is a permanent opposition, a stubborn politics of minority. If a faction could be devised that united republicans from both the degenerate parties, however, it might at least begin to raise the political costs of empire both at home and abroad and

begin to open the way toward a modest revision of our founding charter.

Admittedly, the prospect of a constitutional remedy is
dim. But if we do not at least try to remove the source of the
corruption—the money that drives our politics, the equation
of spending with political speech and voting—then we might
as well give up and join those who ignore politics altogether.
If we shrug and say that the system of corrupt influence can
never be overturned, then we are truly doomed. But if we
are to give up, at least let us avoid the bad faith of pretending
that some attractive and eloquent corporate tool like Obama
might save us.

BARACK OBAMA CAME TO POWER with ambitions to create
another era of good feelings, but he has succeeded only in
reigniting the passions of a long-simmering partisan war that
was sparked by Alexander Hamilton's economic program.
We suffer the passions but lack the principles that animated
the first party system. At least since the age of Jackson, our
politics have been dramatized by actors wearing the costumes
and regalia of Jeffersonian Democracy and the Old Republic even as they have drawn salaries and annuities from one
moneyed interest or another. The similarities between our
current conflicts and such bygone episodes as the debates over
the Bank of the United States and the Panic of 1792 are not
accidental; the great and irresistible engine of government,
the driving power that created the modern state and enabled

America's astonishing rise from colony to global imperium, is finance. Although historians for generations have sneered at their fears and dire prophesies, the old republicans' critique of finance, inherited from Whiggish England and the commonwealth tradition, was *not wrong*—though it was almost from the beginning co-opted, betrayed, and defeated. As Madison foretold, the stockjobbers and their descendants have become "the pretorian band of the Government, at once its tool & its tyrant; bribed by its largesses, & overawing it by clamours & combinations." Hamilton, Madison's principal enemy, is the great prophetic genius of the American System, truly the founding father of our too-big-to-fail despotism. Yet even if the rhetoric of republicanism in American history has very often masked a more mercenary and partial program, that rhetoric remains, for good reason, our native idiom of liberty. But it is more than a vocabulary; it is the philosophical superego to the Hamiltonian ego, the permanent minority report that seeks to hold in check the unbridled hubris of our moneyed interests in all their gaudy diversity.

Let us grant that Barack Obama is as intelligent as his admirers insist. What evidence do we possess that he is also a moral virtuoso? What evidence do we possess that he is a good, a wise, or even a decent man? Yes, he can be eloquent, yet eloquence is no guarantee of wisdom or of virtue. Yes, he has a nice family, but that evinces a private morality. Public morality reveals itself through public action, and all available public evidence points to a man with the character of a common politician, whose singular ambition in life was to attain power; nothing in Barack Obama's political career suggests that he would ever willingly commit himself to a course of action that would cost him an election. His preposterously two-faced approach to Afghanistan is a perfect illustration of his compulsion to split the difference on any given political question—as is the disgraceful inertia of his response to the worst environmental catastrophe in American history. He dillydallies, draws out both friends and opponents, dangles promises in front of everyone, gives a dramatic speech, and then pulls back to gauge the reaction. Since the policy itself is incoherent—and, as usual with Obama, riddled with stipulations and conditions—he can always trim and readjust as necessary. Deadlines and definitions of "combat forces" or "clean-energy future" are infinitely malleable. Since Obama is an intelligent man, surely he understands the meaning of the word *mendacity*.

Having embraced and professionalized the powers of force and fraud previously associated with the likes of John Yoo and Dick Cheney, Obama has embarked on a course of war that will certainly invite further abuses of power. His political survival now depends on martial success in a land that has defeated some of history's most brutal strategies of conquest. Obama has set a trap for himself, but because he is such a clever politician, the spring is just as likely to fall on us instead. Self-styled liberals who defend the Archangel Obama in sickness and in health must now reckon with the realization that their redeemer appears to have moved the Supreme Court farther to the right of where it stood under George W. Bush, at least on the all-important issue of executive power. Obama and his Clintonian advisers now embody the worst traits of both parties. As terrible as the new administration has been with regard to finance and health care, its record on torture, detention, and executive authority is even worse. Obama has institutionalized the usurpations and abuses of the Bush regime; they are now a part of the bipartisan Washington consensus. Our constitutional system may never recover.

Such insidious governance demands serious, sustained opposition, not respectful disagreement or fanciful apologies or mournful lamentations about the tragedy of Obama's presidency. Principles can be sacrificed to hopes as well as to fears.

ACKNOWLEDGMENTS

This book continues an argument that began in the pages of *Harper's Magazine* and would not have been possible without the many contributions of my colleagues and friends at that publication. I am especially grateful to Ben Metcalf, Gemma Sieff, Christian Lorentzen, Donovan Hohn, Paul Ford, Jennifer Szalai, Luke Mitchell, Ken Silverstein, Scott Horton, Bill Wasik, Benjamin Moser, Rafil Kroll-Zaidi, Wyatt Mason, John Sullivan, Ben Austen, Stacey Clarkson, Alyssa Coppelman, Ted Ross, Claire Gutierrez, Sam Stark, Genevieve Smith, Christopher Beha, Rafe Bartholomew, Ellen Rosenbush, Ann Gollin, and Lewis Lapham, who led the way.

I am indebted to Thomas Ferguson, Naomi Klein, John

Berger, William T. Vollmann, and Breyten Breytenbach for their intellectual and moral support. I could not have written this book without the help and guidance of Jin Auh, Scott Moyers, and Tim Duggan. To my parents and to my grandmother and the rest of my family I owe more than I can express. I beg the forgiveness of Deborah, Sebastian, and Wriley, who suffered my monkish confinement with grace and good humor. I will make it up to you.

NOTES

1. The Idea of Influence

7   "the rule of the politician": Joseph Schumpeter, *Capitalism, Socialism, and Democracy* (New York: Harper, 1942).

8   bloc of investors: The investment theory of party competition has been developed above all by Thomas Ferguson, and I am deeply indebted to his work. See his *Golden Rule: The Investment Theory of Party Competition and the Logic of Money-Driven Political Systems* (Chicago, Ill.: University of Chicago Press, 1995).

10   symbolic and empty competition: Ibid., 28.

10   internationalist and capital-intensive firms: These details are found in "From Normalcy to New Deal," ibid., 113–72.

14   who contribute at least $200 to politicians: In 2008, the proportion of the adult U.S. population who contributed at least $200 to political candidates, PACs, or parties was 0.61 percent; the proportion who gave at least $2,300 was 0.13 percent. Most of

the data I cite on lobbying and campaign finance come from the nonpartisan Center for Responsive Politics, Opensecrets.org.

15   a three-part classification of states: James Madison, "Spirit of Governments," *National Gazette*, February 20, 1792, in *The Writings of James Madison*, ed. Gaillard Hunt (New York: Putnam, 1906), Vol. 6, 93.

2. Barack Obama, Inc.

23   were there from the beginning: See Ken Silverstein, "Barack Obama Inc.," *Harper's Magazine*, November 2006.

23   classified by employment affiliation: Federal law prohibits businesses and other organizations from donating directly to candidates; thus employees are routinely pressured by their firms to pitch in and support the company's favorite contender. This regulation conveniently permits firms to plausibly deny official support of any particular candidate and sanctions potentially infinite legal bribery. See Center for Responsive Politics, Open secrets.org.

25   Eventually the bill died of neglect: Mike McIntire, "Nuclear Leaks and Response Tested Obama in Senate," *New York Times*, February 3, 2008.

26   the largest earmark in history: See Timothy P. Carney, *Obamanomics* (Washington, D.C.: Regnery, 2009), 43.

30   the day he was elected senator: See Peter Osnos, "Barack Obama and the Book Business," Century Foundation, October 30, 2006, www.tcf.org.

38   The results were impressive: See Center for Responsive Politics, Opensecrets.org.

39   a little thunderstruck: David S. Broder, "Obama Finds His Address," *Washington Post*, December 23, 2007.

40    $35 million for John Kerry in 2004: David D. Kirkpatrick and Aron Pilhofer, "Finance Filings Offer Glimpses of '08 Candidates," *New York Times*, April 17, 2007; Brian C. Mooney, "Obama Names Spain Ambassador," *Boston Globe*, August 7, 2009.

46   more than twice as much: It's true that 53 percent of Obama's

contributions were under $200, but those contributors are diffuse and unorganized and thus in the current system have no real leverage over a candidate.

47   a staggering 401,194 percent: See "TARP Recipients Paid Out $114 Million for Politicking Last Year," February 4, 2009, Opensecrets.org.

48   paying for mere crumbs: Labor's poor returns on investment offers strong evidence of what is called the iceberg theory, according to which the threat of contributing to a political rival is more influential than are actual contributions. See Marcos Chamon and Ethan Kaplan, "The Iceberg Theory of Campaign Contributions: Political Threats and Interest Group Behavior," unpublished paper, April 2007.

50   various and sundry lobbyists: See David D. Kirkpatrick, "In Transition, Ties to Lobbying," *New York Times*, November 14, 2008.

51   deals involving Democratic donors: See Carney, *Obamanomics*, 20–25; and Michael Luo, "In Banking, Emanuel Made Money and Connections," *New York Times*, December 4, 2008. For contributions, see Center for Responsive Politics, Opensecrets .org.

53   "a lot of helpful work": Ceci Connolly, Joe Stephens, and R. Jeffrey Smith, "Daschle Delayed Revealing Tax Glitch," *Washington Post*, February 1, 2009.

3. A Parable of Peaches

59   was invented in the 1980s by Democrats: See Robert G. Kaiser, *So Damn Much Money: The Triumph of Lobbying and the Corrosion of American Government* (New York: Vintage, 2009).

66   a $200 million lobbying campaign: Joseph E. Stiglitz, *Freefall: America, Free Markets, and the Sinking of the World Economy* (New York: Norton, 2009), 162.

66   "we have decided that freedom is the answer": Stephen Labaton, "Congress Passes Wide-Ranging Bill Easing Bank Laws," *New York Times*, November 5, 1999.

67   the unforgettable FELINE PRIDES: See Frank Partnoy, *Infec-

tious Greed: How Deceit and Risk Corrupted the Financial Markets (New York: Times Books, 2003), 204–22.

68   "It would have been inappropriate": Joseph Kahn, "Former Treasury Secretary Joins Leadership Triangle at Citigroup," *New York Times*, October 27, 1999.

70   broad legal exemption to many derivatives: Partnoy, *Infectious Greed*, 44ff, 145.

73   "the effect on already disrupted markets could be vast": Dan Froomkin discusses these passages in "Rubin: I Actually Supported Regulating Derivatives," *Huffington Post*, April 20, 2010.

4. Buyer Beware

83   this decision was especially ironic: For the shadow bailout and its single-payer consequences, see Thomas Ferguson and Robert Johnson, "Too Big to Bail: The 'Paulson Put,' Presidential Politics, and the Global Financial Meltdown," parts 1 and 2, *International Journal of Political Economy*, Vol. 38, Nos. 1 and 2 (spring and summer 2009). See also Dean Baker, *Plunder and Blunder: The Rise and Fall of the Bubble Economy* (New York: Polipoint, 2008), 107–17.

85   the New Deal cost a mere $500 billion: Statement of Neil Barofsky, special inspector general, Troubled Asset Relief Program, before the House Committee on Financial Services Subcommittee on Oversight and Investigations, July 22, 2009. See also Eamon Javers, "Bailouts Could Cost U.S. $23 Trillion," *Politico*, July 20, 2009.

86   a simple two-page form: See Matt Kapp, "The Annotated TARP Application," June 30, 2009, VanityFair.com.

87   the hard teachings of Machiavelli: *Discourses*, Book I, chap. 3, "What Events Caused Tribunes of the People to Be Established in Rome—A Thing That Made the State More Perfect," in *Machiavelli: The Chief Works and Others*, trans. Allan Gilbert (Durham, N.C.: Duke University Press, 1989), Vol. 1, 201.

89   helped inflate the bubble: See Yves Smith, *ECONNED: How Unenlightened Self-Interest Damaged Democracy and Corrupted Capitalism* (New York: Palgrave Macmillan, 2010), 231–67, espe-

cially her discussion of the Magnetar hedge fund. See also Jesse Eisinger and Jake Bernstein, "The Magnetar Trade: How One Hedge Fund Helped Keep the Bubble Going," April 9, 2010, ProPublica.org.

89   the continued corrupt influence of America's economic royalists: See John T. Flynn, "The Marines Land in Wall Street," *Harper's Magazine*, July 1934.

93   "but this time in a faster car": Office of the Special Inspector General for the Troubled Asset Relief Program, Quarterly Report to Congress, January 30, 2010, 8ff, www.Sigtarp.gov.

95   about $19 million a day: All lobbying figures are from the Center for Responsive Politics, Opensecrets.org.

95   was still flowing into the accounts of Democrats: As of May 16—see Michael Becker, "Reversing 2009 Trend, Business Money Now Flowing More to Republicans," May 25, 2010, Center for Responsive Politics, Opensecrets.org.

95   Until their power is broken: Simon Johnson has made this point repeatedly since the crisis began. See his blog at Baseline scenario.com and his contribution to the Roosevelt Foundation's conference of March 3, 2010, Make Markets Be Markets, Make marketsbemarkets.org. In *13 Bankers: The Wall Street Takeover and the Next Financial Meltdown* (New York: Pantheon, 2010), which appeared as I was completing work on this book, Johnson and his coauthor James Kwak frame their analysis of the crisis with a discussion of the Jeffersonian critique of finance.

97   Banks would necessarily become relatively small and dull again. See, for example, L. Randall Wray, "Bye-Bye to Bernanke's 'Insidious Banks': End 'Too Big to Fail' in 2 Easy Steps," Roosevelt Institute, March 22, 2010, NewDeal20.org. See also Stiglitz, *Freefall*; the presentations collected by the Roosevelt Institute at Makemarketsbemarkets.org; and Simon Johnson's writings noted above.

5. Monsters of Sedition

100   countless revolutionary and postrevolutionary polemics: See Caroline Robbins, *The Eighteenth-Century Commonwealthman*

(Cambridge, Mass.: Harvard University Press, 1959); Bernard Bailyn, *The Ideological Origins of the American Revolution* (Cambridge, Mass.: Harvard University Press, 1967); J.G.A. Pocock, *The Machiavellian Moment* (Princeton, N.J.: Princeton University Press, 1979); Gordon S. Wood, *The Creation of the American Republic* (Chapel Hill: University of North Carolina Press, 1969); Lance Banning, *The Jeffersonian Persuasion* (Ithaca, N.Y.: Cornell University Press, 1978).

101   wealth and war-making power: Banning, *The Jeffersonian Persuasion*, 47; Gordon S. Wood, *Empire of Liberty* (New York: Oxford University Press, 2009), 93.

101   "alter its nature, though not its name": John Trenchard and Thomas Gordon, *Cato's Letters: or, Essays on Liberty, Civil and Religious, and Other Important Subjects* (Indianapolis, Ind.: Liberty Fund, 1995), Vol. 2, no. 91, 648.

102   "a precarious, uncertain, and transitory value": Ibid., Vol. 2, No. 107, 757–58.

103   and tyranny, oligarchy, or anarchy results: James Harrington, *The Commonwealth of Oceana and A System of Politics*, ed. J.G.A. Pocock (New York: Cambridge University Press, 1992), 271–72.

104   did not impose order on the monetary system: Bray Hammond, *Banks and Politics in America from the Revolution to the Civil War* (Princeton, N.J.: Princeton University Press, 1957), 89.

106   to prevent their enactment: Ibid., 116; Charles Beard, *The Economic Origins of Jeffersonian Democracy* (New York: Macmillan, 1915); Charles Beard, *The American Party Battle* (New York: Macmillan, 1928); Lance Banning, *The Sacred Fire of Liberty: James Madison and the Founding of the Federal Republic* (Ithaca, N.Y.: Cornell University Press, 1995).

106   a confection spun out of nothingness: See J.G.A. Pocock, *Virtue, Commerce, and History* (New York: Cambridge University Press, 1985).

106   the law had not yet caught up with their innovations: Hammond, *Banks and Politics*, 105.

107   a political dialectic that has continued to the present day: Ibid., 118–22; Beard, *Economic Origins*, 109.

109 "corruptions of a stale and pampered monarchy": William Branch Giles, Speech in the House of Representatives on the Apportionment Bill, April 9, 1792, in Lance Banning, ed., *Liberty and Order: The First American Party Struggle* (Indianapolis, Ind.: Liberty Fund, 2004), 108–9.

110 "In every political society, parties are unavoidable": (*The Writings of James Madison*, ed. Gaillard Hunt (New York: Putnam, 1900), Vol. 6, 86.

112 the very model of the corrupt government official: Most of the details presented here of William Duer's adventures in finance and his role in creating the Panic of 1792 are drawn from Robert F. Jones, *The King of the Alley* (Philadelphia, Pa.: American Philosophical Society, 1992).

113 published under the name Philo-Publius: Banning, *Sacred Fire*, 196; Jones, *King of the Alley*, 111–12.

114 He was the father of the revolving door: Jones, *King of the Alley*, 114–33; John Steele Gordon, "The Great Crash (of 1792)," *American Heritage*, May/June 1999.

114 those options had appreciated by 1,200 percent: Jones, *King of the Alley*, 159–60, 168–69, 170–73.

116 credit contracted severely, and the bubble burst: Ibid., 174ff; Gordon, "The Great Crash."

116 "could not have done so much evil": Jones, *King of the Alley*, 188–91.

116 "The stocksellers say he will rise again": To Thomas Mann Randolph, March 16, 1792, *Works of Jefferson*, Vol. 6, ed. Paul Leicester Ford (New York: Putnam, 1904).

117 "they are afraid to make any new money arrangements": To Thomas Mann Randolph, April 19, 1792, ibid.

117 half of which was used to manage the market: Jones, *King of the Alley*, 200.

119 Ultimately, they made a bad bet: Wood, *Empire of Liberty*, 168–73.

119 The government prepared lists of foreigners for deportation: Ibid., 250–60.

120 Most of the others who were convicted: Ibid., 250–70.

121 "Let us not establish a tyranny": *The Works of Alexander Ham-*

ilton, ed. Henry Cabot Lodge, Federal Edition, 12 vols. (New York: Putnam, 1904), Vol. 10. Emphasis in original.

121   to finance the debt resulting from the War of 1812: See Hammond, *Banks and Politics*, 145; Banning, *Jeffersonian Persuasion*, 127.

122   virtues of private life and personal cultivation: See Pocock, *Virtue, Commerce, and History*; J.G.A. Pocock, *Barbarism and Religion* (New York: Cambridge University Press, 1999), Vol. 1, 101–10.

123   Madison was also a close reader of Hume and Smith: See Douglass Adair, "That Politics May Be Reduced to a Science: David Hume, James Madison, and the Tenth Federalist" and "The Tenth Federalist Revisited," in *Fame and the Founding Fathers: Essays by Douglass Adair* (New York: Norton, 1974). For the critique of classical virtue, see Paul A. Rahe, *Republics Ancient and Modern* (Chapel Hill: University of North Carolina Press, 1994), Vol. 3.

124   "the term monarchy cannot apply": *The Works of Alexander Hamilton*, Vol. 1, Speeches in the Federal Convention, para. 1037.

124   Even if we grant that Hamilton personally was a kind of incorruptible saint: Banning, *Jeffersonian Persuasion*, 139.

126   without violating the rights of property: Ibid., 204–5.

126   He distrusted any interest that might grow so powerful as to overawe all others: "The power of granting charters, he observed, is a great and important power, and ought not to be exercised unless we find ourselves expressly authorized to grant them. Here he dilated on the great and extensive influence that incorporated societies had on public affairs in Europe. They are powerful machines, which have always been found competent to effect objects on principles in a great measure independent of the people." *Writings of James Madison*, Vol. 6, Speeches in the First Congress—Third Session, 1791.

6. The Greatest Wealth Is Health

136   "I'd be delighted to sit down and compare my IQ to yours": Meghan Clyne, "A Little Learning . . . Is a Bidenesque Thing," *Weekly Standard*, December 21, 2009. It wasn't the first time that Biden had quoted "the classic poet, Virgil."

138   The liberal press dutifully played its role: David Leonhardt,

"In Health Bill, Obama Attacks Wealth Inequality," *New York Times*, March 23, 2010. Leonhardt published a similar laudation after the passage of the Senate financial reform bill: "Congress and the White House have completed 16 months of activity that rival any other since the New Deal in scope or ambition." Again, Leonhardt insisted that Obama's aim was "to try to lift economic growth while also reducing income inequality." Remarkably, he offered not one shred of evidence that the bills passed by the Obama Democrats would do anything to reduce income inequality. Instead, the piece was a tissue of assertions, duly supported by quotations from credentialed authorities, that the bills really were significant, important, and surprising. See David Leonhardt, "A Progressive Agenda to Remake Washington," *New York Times*, May 21, 2010.

139   or that they will really end up paying those taxes: The phenomenon of "elasticity of taxable income," an economic concept well-known to Obama's advisers and to David Leonhardt, will no doubt erase significant portions of the projected income from these modest tax increases. See Emmanuel Saez, Joel B. Slemrod, and Seth H. Giertz, "The Elasticity of Taxable Income with Respect to Marginal Tax Rates: A Critical Review," Working Paper 15012, National Bureau of Economic Research, May 2009.

139   drew heavily on ideas from the right-wing Heritage Foundation: Jane Hamsher, "Pelosi: Heritage Foundation Designed Health Care Bill," March 24, 2010, Firedoglake.com; E. J. Dionne, "Why Democrats Are Fighting for a Republican Health Plan," *Washington Post*, March 19, 2010.

141   Baucus's draft bill was reportedly leaked to lobbyists: See Paul Blumenthal, "What's Up with the Baucus Bill?" September 9, 2009, Sunlightfoundation.com.

142   "two former chiefs of staff to Max Baucus": Paul Blumenthal, "The Legacy of Billy Tauzin: The White House-PhRMA Deal," February 12, 2010, Sunlightfoundation.com.

142   The health industry as a whole spent $545 million lobbying congress in 2009: Center for Responsive Politics, Opensecrets.org.

143 "tax money will have to be found to keep the jalopy on the road": Holman W. Jenkins, Jr., "Now, Can We Have Health-Care Reform?" *Wall Street Journal*, March 24, 2010.

145 make their money by keeping sick people out of their pools: See Marshall Auerback and L. Randall Wray, "Toward True Health Care Reform: More Care, Less Insurance," Public Policy Brief, Levy Economics Institute of Bard College, No. 110, 2010, Levyinstitute.org.

148 such perfectly sensible business decisions: Robert Pear, "Coverage Now for Sick Children? Check Fine Print," *New York Times*, March 28, 2010.

150 During the final weeks of the election: Casey Ross, "Financial Executives Spent Big on Brown," *Boston Globe*, February 1, 2010.

150 compared with 8 percent in 2009: Brian C. Mooney, "Outside Donations Buoyed Brown," *Boston Globe*, February 24, 2010.

150 As Tom Ferguson and Jie Chen showed: Thomas Ferguson and Jie Chen, "1, 2, 3, Many Tea Parties? A Closer Look at the 2010 Massachusetts Senate Race," Roosevelt Institute, April 14, 2010, Newdeal20.org.

151 unemployment rates remained very high: Bureau of Labor Statistics, Regional and State Employment and Unemployment Summary, May 21, 2010.

7. Rise of the Pseudo-Cons

153 figures such as John Lukacs: John Lukacs, "The American Conservatives," *Harper's Magazine*, January 1984.

157 "the supreme form of generosity": José Ortega y Gasset, *The Revolt of the Masses* (New York: Norton, 1994), 76.

159 the long right turn: The best account is Thomas Ferguson and Joel Rogers, *Right Turn: The Decline of the Democrats and the Future of American Politics* (New York: Hill and Wang, 1986).

162 as an obstacle to their ambitions: Hammond, *Banks and Politics in America*, 333–42; Ferguson, *Golden Rule*, 55–61.

163 Jacksonian Democracy gave birth to the modern political machine: Hammond, *Banks and Politics in America* 336–39; Fer-

guson, *Golden Rule*, 59–60; James W. Ceaser, "Demagoguery, Statesmanship, and Presidential Politics," in *The Constitutional Presidency*, ed. Joseph M. Bessette and Jeffrey K. Tulis (Baltimore, Md.: Johns Hopkins University Press, 2009).

164   "it may be well to send me the usual retainers": Arthur M. Schlesinger Jr., *The Age of Jackson* (New York: Little, Brown, 1945), 84. Emphasis in original.

165   with diabolical skill neutralized and absorbed: Walter Karp, *The Politics of War* (New York: Harper and Row, 1979, republished by Franklin Square, 2003); Ferguson, *Golden Rule*, 77–78.

165   Aristocracy, plutocracy, oligarchy: See Kevin Phillips, *Wealth and Democracy: A Political History of the American Rich* (New York: Broadway, 2002).

167   his formerly reluctant and highly selective approach to trust-busting: Karp, *Politics of War*, 130–45.

168   a timid follower of political convention: See Kevin Baker, "Barack Hoover Obama," *Harper's Magazine*, July 2009.

168   new laws to legitimize their business activities: Karp, *Politics of War*, 144–72.

8. The Long Emergency

178   Only Justice Antonin Scalia accepted the theory: See Karl Manheim and Allen Ides, "The Unitary Executive," Legal Studies Paper No. 2006–39, November 2006.

182   the Justice Department itself was transformed: Scott Horton, "State of Exception: Bush's War on the Rule of Law," *Harper's Magazine*, July 2007; "Vote Machine: How Republicans Hacked the Justice Department," *Harper's Magazine*, March 2008; "Justice after Bush: Prosecuting an Outlaw Administration," *Harper's Magazine,* December 2008; "The Guantánamo Suicides: A Camp Delta Sergeant Blows the Whistle," *Harper's Magazine*, March 2010. See also Horton's legal affairs blog, No Comment, Harpers.org.

183   Not for long: See Charlie Savage, "To Critics, Obama's Terror Policy Looks a Lot Like Bush's," *New York Times*, July 2, 2009.

188   which included slicing his genitals with a scalpel: See Glenn

Greenwald, "Obama Administration Threatens Britain to Keep Torture Evidence Concealed," May 12, 2009, Salon.com.

190   Kagan endorsed the view: Charlie Savage, "Obama's War on Terror May Resemble Bush's in Some Areas," *New York Times*, February 17, 2009.

191   Given the escalation in Afghanistan: "The President's Dilemma: Deficits, Debt, and U.S. Defense Spending," Project on Defense Alternatives, Commonwealth Institute, Cambridge, Mass., January 18, 2010.

191   as of May 2010 there were 92,000: May was the first month since the war began in which the number of troops in Afghanistan officially surpassed the number in Iraq. Brookings Institution, *Iraq Index*, May 25, 2010, 20.

193   Obama made a tactical retreat: Charlie Savage, "Obama Takes New Route to Opposing Parts of Laws," *New York Times*, January 8, 2010.

195   forms of abuse continue to take place in the secret jail: Alissa J. Rubin, "Afghans Detail Detention in 'Black Jail' at U.S. Base," *New York Times*, November 28, 2009.

196   including many of the Predator drone attacks: Jeremy Scahill, "The Secret U.S. War in Pakistan," *Nation*, November 23, 2009.

197   the administration's refusal to justify the program was untenable: Jane Mayer, "The Predator War," *New Yorker*, October 16, 2009.

197   an American citizen named Anwar al-Awlaki: See Dana Priest, "U.S. Military Teams, Intelligence Deeply Involved in Aiding Yemen on Strikes," *Washington Post*, January 27, 2010; Glenn Greenwald, "Presidential Assassinations of U.S. Citizens," January 27, 2010, Salon.com.

9. Speak, Money

201   "on the terms of the liberalism it displaces": Schlesinger, *The Age of Jackson*, 391.

207   the absence of an arbitrary or dominating will: My discussion of the republican theory of liberty draws especially on Philip Pettit, *Republicanism: A Theory of Freedom and Government* (New

York: Oxford University Press, 1997); and Quentin Skinner, *Liberty before Liberalism* (New York: Cambridge University Press, 1997).

207 slavish and cringing dependents: Skinner, *Liberty before Liberalism*, 94.

208 particularly skilled in the arts of flattery and ingratiation: Pettit, *Republicanism*, 25.

208 "Liberty is, to live upon one's own Terms": Trenchard and Gordon, "An Inquiry into the Nature and Extent of Liberty; with Its Loveliness and Advantages, and the Vile Effects of Slavery," *Cato's Letters*, No. 62, 430.

213 paid no federal taxes: Christopher Helman, "What the Top U.S. Companies Pay in Taxes," April 1, 2010, Forbes.com; Lynnley Browning, "Study Tallies Corporations Not Paying Income Tax," *New York Times*, August 12, 2008.

216 total share of income: Emmanuel Saez, "Striking It Richer: The Evolution of Top Incomes in the United States," updated with 2007 figures, August 5, 2009, 6, fig. 1. My discussion of income inequality relies on the figures presented in this article and in Thomas Piketty and Emmanuel Saez, "Income Inequality in the United States, 1913–1998," *Quarterly Journal of Economics*, Vol. 118, No. 1 (2003), 1–39. Saez updates income figures annually and makes them available in Excel format on his Web page at http://elsa.berkeley.edu/~saez. As of this writing, the most recent figures were for 2007; figures for 2008 will be made available by the IRS in August 2010.

217 a *190 percent rise* in real income: Piketty and Saez explain that this calculation is pretax and excludes capital gains, noncash fringe benefits, and government payments such as Social Security and unemployment benefits. The year 1973 represents an apex in the income of the bottom 99 percent that was not surpassed until 1997; over that same period, the top 1 percent saw more than 100 percent income growth.

218 under the Bush expansion the superrich captured 65 percent: Saez, "Striking It Richer," 9, table 1.

218 ephemeral antagonisms over God, gays, or guns: See Larry Bartels, *Unequal Democracy: The Political Economy of the New Gilded*

Notes

Age (Princeton, N.J.: Princeton University Press, 2008), 83–90; and Andrew Gelman, *Red State Blue State, Rich State Poor State* (Princeton, N.J.: Princeton University Press, 2010).

218   almost all Americans are better off economically under Democrats: *Unequal Democracy*, 33, fig. 2.1.

219   lower-income voters are more sensitive: Ibid., 113–15.

219   each additional dollar spent per voter: Ibid., 118–20.

220   "Democracy is premised on responsiveness": *Citizens United v. Federal Election Commission*, 43–44 (Justice Anthony Kennedy, quoting his own dissenting opinion in *McConnell v. Federal Election Commission*).

221   virtue for us is no more than a spotless credit rating: See Pocock, *Machiavellian Moment*, 456.

10. Inventions of Prudence

226   an initiative for a constitutional convention: See FixCongress-First.org and CallAConvention.com.

227   taller than the common citizen: A rigorous system would ban all contributions and thus would destroy the parties, which like business corporations subsist on a steady diet of cash and can be kept alive on nothing else. The fact that a reform would kill the parties is not necessarily an objection, however. The parties have no constitutional sanction. They are, however, an essential element of our shadow constitution and for that reason alone deserve to be put to death.

228   to contain the power of the rich: John P. McCormick, "Contain the Wealthy and Patrol the Magistrates: Restoring Elite Accountability to Popular Government," *American Political Science Review*, Vol. 100, No. 2 (May 2006), 147–63.

INDEX

Index

political will and self-interest,
228–230
constraints, freedom conceived as
absence of, 205–214
Coolidge, Calvin, 169
corporations
paying no income tax, 213–214
political contributions and influence
of, 219–223
political contributions and role in
government, 7–11, 14–17
rights of personhood and, 221,
225
Countrywide Financial, 92
Craig, Gregory, 131, 192
credit, historical U.S. conflicts over
finance and, 99–127
Constitution and early economic
programs, 104–112
Duer's market speculation and,
112–117
economic interests and vision of
the state, 118–127
ideological origins of American
Revolution and, 100–104

Daley, Richard M., 51
Daschle, Linda Hall, 52
Daschle, Tom, 38, 51–53
deficit spending, 173–176
Defoe, Daniel, 122
democracy
America's mythological narrative
of, 4–6
capitalism and corruption of, 14–17
capitalism and economic model of,
6–11
Madison's concept of interest and,
11–14
Democratic Party
foreign policy and imperialism,
165–172
history of, 161–165
ideological incoherence of, 153–160
income levels of voters and,
218–219
interests and, 9–11, 160–164
Obama on, 35
political contributions to, 96
derivatives
Commodities Futures
Modernization Act and, 73–75

Commodity Futures Trading
Commission and, 69–73
financial crisis and, 87–90
financial reform legislation and,
90–98
Dionne, E. J., 139
Dodd, Christopher, 158
contributions to, 51
financial reform legislation and,
90–92, 96
Drake, Thomas, 194
drone attacks, under Obama, 196–197
Duane, William, 120
Duer, Kitty, 113
Duer, William, 112–117
Duncan, Arne, 48
Durbin, Dick, 38

earmarks, 59
economic libertarians, 86–87
economic policies, of Obama
as expressed in *The Audacity of
Hope,* 55–65, 75–80
influences on, 25, 53, 55
Edwards, John, 30
Eisenhower, Dwight D., 175
election of 2008
Biden and, 43–44
contributions to Obama campaign,
39–42, 44–49
Obama's policy messages during,
35–39, 42–43
Emanuel, Rahm, 50–51, 130–131
Employee Free Choice Act, 48
Enroll America, 141
Enron, 70, 75, 88
Espionage Act, 169
Ethics in Government Act, 178
Exelon Corporation, 24, 25, 49
extraordinary rendition, 183–184,
195

Fair Elections Now, 226
Fannie Mae, 83, 84, 85
"federalist," 202
Federalist Party, 12, 107–110, 113,
118–121, 161, 163–164
Federal Reserve, financial crisis and,
82–84
Federal Reserve Act, 169
Feingold, Russell D., 67
Ferguson, Thomas, 7, 150